THE

THE USES
OF ENGLISH

THE USES OF ENGLISH

GUIDELINES FOR THE TEACHING OF ENGLISH FROM THE ANGLO-AMERICAN CONFERENCE AT DARTMOUTH COLLEGE

HERBERT J. MULLER

Indiana University

Holt, Rinehart and Winston, Inc.

New York · Chicago · San Francisco · Atlanta · Dallas
Montreal · Toronto · London

The Anglo-American Seminar at Dartmouth College was cosponsored by the Modern Language Association of America, the National Association for the Teaching of English (United Kingdom), and the National Council of Teachers of English. The seminar was supported by a grant from the Carnegie Corporation of New York.

Library of Congress Catalog Card Number: 67-24782

2657955
2657906

Printed in the United States of America
1   2   3   4   5   6   7   8   9

PREFACE

In the late summer of 1966, some fifty assorted educators met at Dartmouth College to hold the Anglo-American
Seminar on the Teaching of English—the first large-scale
international conference on this basic subject. They were
well assorted because they had been carefully selected to
assure diversity of experience, interest, and point of view.
Some were teachers in primary and secondary schools, others
teachers in schools of education, still others university professors concerned about what has been going on in the
schools. They included specialists in the various branches
of English, such as literature, linguistics, creative writing,
rhetoric, and the skills of communication. A dozen or so
other specialists, including psychologists and sociologists,
visited the seminar as consultants. But underlying all such
professional differences—not to mention those between all
the unique individuals—were the basic differences between

the school systems and traditions of Great Britain and the United States. The members of the seminar were evenly divided between British and Americans, with the addition of an occasional Canadian, and they soon discovered that often they were not talking the same language. So they settled down to an international dialogue, which went on for four weeks. During this time they lived and sipped together, met daily to thrash out their differences over a score of issues. Finally, after much amicable confusion and debate, they arrived at a surprising measure of agreement about what is wrong with the teaching of English and what ought to be done about it.

This book is a report on the proceedings of the seminar, designed for the general reader. (John Dixon of England has written a report addressed to the professional community.) Inasmuch as the discussions ranged all over a large subject and produced dozens of papers on different topics, my account is highly selective. I have skimmed over some problems that interest chiefly specialists. But I owe some further explanations to the general reader too.

One reason I was asked to write this book was an odd qualification. I knew little about the teaching of English in the elementary and secondary schools, which was the primary concern of the seminar, and had taken only a casual interest in it. It was thought that I would therefore be uncommitted, unprejudiced. I soon lost this possible virtue, however, as I found the discussions uncommonly stimulating and realized more fully the importance of the issues at stake. Although I have reported in the guise of a detached observer, I should emphasize that all these issues are highly debatable (a gentle way of saying "controversial"—a word frightening to some Americans) and that I am not in fact uncommitted or free from bias. Naturally I have tried to do justice to the different opinions expressed, but I have not tried to write a wholly impersonal report. While obliged in any case to select and interpret what seemed to me the most important questions raised at the seminar, I have felt free to add some commentary. Often I deliberately introduce the first person to make clear that I am expressing my own opinion, but also to remind the reader that it is an opinion and therefore debatable.

I am pleased to express my indebtedness to all the participants in the seminar, from whom—after some forty years of teaching English—I learned a good deal. In the same spirit I regret burying so many lively, genial people in a blanket acknowledgment. My debt is not adequately acknowledged in the text either, since I thought it better in this condensed report for a nonprofessional audience not to identify all the speakers in discussions. For the most part I have cited names only when quoting from papers written for the seminar. In warmly thanking the anonymous many whose contributions to this book are not specified, I should add that I have done nothing like full justice to anyone. I make partial amends by listing, at the end of the book, the names and positions of all participants and consultants.

H. J. M.

Bloomington, Indiana
July 1967

CONTENTS

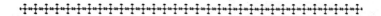

CHAPTER ONE

WHAT IS ENGLISH?

Offhand, everybody knows what English is. It is the language we have been using all our lives, it is reading and writing, it is what we all studied for years in school—grammar and spelling, composition and literature. Everybody seems to agree too that it is the most fundamental subject, inasmuch as it is the only one required of all students throughout their school years; all are obviously dependent on their command of the language for both their learning and their living purposes. But here is the beginning of much trouble. Nobody is likely to think hard about something that everybody takes for granted. Until recent years educators gave remarkably little attention to this most fundamental subject in the curriculum, even though it was plain that after all those years in school most young people could not read, write, or speak well. For such reasons the Anglo-American

Seminar opened and ended its discussions with the seemingly elementary question: What is English?

The immediate answer appeared to be that it is a state of hopeless confusion, and teaching it, as someone has said, is "not a profession but a predicament." To begin with, English is perforce what English teachers teach; and just what have they been teaching? In America the answer must include a fantastic hodgepodge, ranging from journalism, play production, business letters, research techniques, use of the library, and proper study habits to orientation to school life, career counseling, use of the telephone, and advice on dating —almost anything beyond toilet training. In California 217 different courses have been classified as English by the state department of education. Albert Kitzhaber observed that with the possible exception of what are known in America as "social studies" (or what David Riesman calls "social slops"), English is the least clearly defined subject in the curriculum. Teachers of mathematics or geography who wander from their subject are aware that they are doing so, "but an English teacher can teach almost anything without anyone, including the teacher, realizing that it is no longer English that is being taught." Anything that anyone thinks is good for youngsters can be dumped into the course because it involves some use of language.

Yet this only forces the question what English "really" is or should be. Although there is general agreement on some fundamentals, such as literature and composition, these raise further questions about specific aims and priorities. Kitzhaber also observed that there is no generally accepted philosophy to guide decisions about what the study should be centered on, what should be its primary aims— not to mention how best to achieve those aims. Thoughtful young high school teachers who visited the seminar said they wanted most of all advice on what they should be doing, and why.

Thus English invariably includes literature, which many

4

teachers regard as the very heart of their subject. All English departments in the colleges and universities make the study of literature their main business. Nevertheless the ordinary citizen regards it as only a kind of elegant pastime, not really essential to an education. Those who think otherwise are therefore under more pressure to decide on the critical questions: What kind of literature should be taught, and for what purpose? Should the primary aim be proficiency in reading, a basic skill all students should have? Or the enjoyment of good literature, which too many lack in an age of television? Or knowledge of our literary heritage, which the colleges put first?

Other teachers believe that English should be centered on language—the understanding, manipulation, and appreciation of language. Here the ordinary citizen is likely to agree on the practical importance of writing and speaking well, but teachers may be troubled by other questions. In composition, which is always taught, should priority be given to expository, functional writing or to personal, imaginative writing? While the former may seem more useful, many who go no further than high school will do little writing of any kind after they leave except personal letters, and most will certainly not write themes or essays. The ability to talk fluently and effectively would seem more important, but for some reason talking is not taught in most English classes; in America it is another subject, usually optional, called "speech." Or if one considers more broadly "the skills of communication," the fashionable phrase today, what about subject matter or intellectual content? Training in rhetoric, logical thinking, and critical analysis? Advertisers appear to be quite skillful in communicating, selling people on the virtues of their wares, but one may doubt that their art is an appropriate study for an English course—except perhaps as an exercise in propaganda analysis, a safeguard against the common abuses of the power of language.

Another problem raised by language is the teaching of

"good English," which has always meant primarily correct English. It has long made grammar a staple of the English curriculum. Readers who remember unhappily all the exercises they had to do in grammar, syntax, diagraming sentences, and the like may be more depressed by the word now going around, that the conventional grammar taught in our schools is mostly obsolete, and that at best all those exercises helped little if any in improving their writing. But now teachers may wonder about the new science of linguistics, which among other things is producing new grammars while making the study of English more respectable in an age dominated by science. How much does this up-to-date grammar help in reading or writing? Or need one worry about such questions? Since language is the means by which man carries on all his distinctive activities, should it not be taught as a humanistic study, worth knowing about—like literature —even if it has no immediate practical value? Should not English make more of its own distinctive content as a part of our rich heritage, and resist the tendency to make it chiefly a service department, teaching useful skills? Or perhaps just emphasize that it can be satisfying for its own sake —even be fun?

The important thing, at any rate, is not the different answers that are being given to all such questions. It is that the questions are being asked, more persistently than ever before. They reflect an intense dissatisfaction in the leaders of the profession. The search for a "philosophy" is itself significant, for this is something traditionalists usually can get along without; all they need is some resounding phrases, like "our great literary heritage," to dignify the customary ways of teaching. The Anglo-American Seminar that met to wrestle with these questions grew out of a concerted movement to improve the teaching of English that got under way in America six or eight years ago, and in Great Britain more recently. The English departments in universities, traditionally devoted to turning out scholars or literary critics, are at last beginning to pay some attention to the preparation of students for teaching, a problem that had been left to departments of education more interested in methodology than either literature or language. In America two dozen Curriculum Study Centers have been set up in universities to work out coherent, cumulative, purposeful curriculums in English from grade school through to the end of high school.

An immediate reason for the tardy recognition that English is being taught poorly was the stimulus of the "new mathematics" and the "new science" in American schools. Some educators naturally concluded that there ought to be a "new English" to match. Another professional stimulus was the work of linguists, who were discrediting old methods by their scientific studies of language. But more important was the "education explosion" since the last World War, especially in America, which has made education a major industry and front-page news. Whereas in 1900 only one out of ten American young people went to high school, and one out of twenty-five to college, mostly from middle- and upper-class homes accustomed to "good English," an affluent society is now sending the great majority to high school and is flooding the colleges with millions of all kinds of students. There are today almost a million teachers of English, 100,000 of them in the high schools. When the hordes of students began crowding the high schools, these had to deal with large numbers who were not much interested in academic work or clearly up to it; as John Fisher wrote, "A high school program had to be devised that could be taught by inferior teachers to uninterested students under impossible working conditions." Now that more than half of these students are going on to college, the old program will no longer do.

Mass education is in turn but one effect of the social revolution, or cluster of revolutions, that in all the advanced countries has been creating a predominantly urban, technological society and an extraordinarily rapid pace of change.

7

Another effect is the "communications revolution," including the growth of the new mass media—radio and television—that compete with the schools. Still another is the "knowledge explosion," which has created the basic problem of maintaining communications among the educated, the countless specialists in science and technology; thousands of technical journals are unreadable for all but specialists. The seminar was most concerned about a particular problem accentuated by increasing affluence, the handicaps of millions of youngsters brought up in "disadvantaged areas"—the polite terms for slums and minority ghettos—where Standard English amounts to a foreign dialect. Altogether, literary people habitually complain of our "standardized mass society"; but for educators the problem is that it is also by far the most heterogeneous, fluid society in all history.

Now, it should be said at once that the seminar did not come out with a revolutionary new English. At the outset one of its originators expressed the hope that there would be radical disagreement, even some loose ends left hanging; and this hope was not disappointed. Some participants were soon oppressed by the sense of frustration and futility normal to this age of incessant committees, conferences, and conventions, in which language is discharging most faithfully its functions of disguising thought and preventing silence. At least one took a desperate view of the state of English, saying that the subject was dying or dead, in effect just live enough to serve as another "crisis" in an age of perpetual crisis. Yet he too was pleased by the measure of consensus that the seminar finally arrived at. Controversy often obscured the obvious fact that from the beginning almost all the participants substantially agreed on what is wrong with most teaching of English in the schools. More surprising, at the end most endorsed a number of recommendations that would be revolutionary enough if put into effect.

These will be the subject of the following chapters.

8

Meanwhile I should also say at once that I am reporting as one who had taken for granted that the seminar would not reach agreement on an ideal new curriculum, and that it should not. No group could ever lay down a completely satisfactory program in any subject, least of all English, for a generation to come. To my mind the disagreements were as fruitful as the final agreements. They at least clarified the basic issues and the reasons why these can never be resolved for good. They demonstrated that there is still plenty of life in the subject and in the profession. If they left English in some confusion, they recalled the ferment of recent times, the widespread, often imaginative, sometimes exciting efforts to improve the teaching of it. And the confusion itself recalled changes in education that have been going on for a long time now, to some welcome effects. Dartmouth College, the host of the seminar, could serve to illustrate historical gains that harried teachers may overlook. I was told that when it was founded in the eighteenth century, authorized by a royal charter to teach "Indians and others," it offered the hapless Indians only Greek, Latin, Hebrew, and religion.

More specifically, the disagreements grew out of the complexity of the problems besetting the profession. This report might be justified if it gives readers nothing but a fuller awareness of the complexities, which in any case they should be warned they will meet to the bitter end. In his influential book *The Process of Education,* Jerome Bruner wrote that "the curriculum of a subject should be determined by the most fundamental understanding that can be achieved of the underlying principles that give structure to that subject." The new mathematics and new science are built on such structural principles. Frank Whitehead of England accordingly raised the question whether this concept of structure could be applied to English in any but a loose metaphorical sense. Linguists answered that it can be applied to the study of language, and some literary critics (such as Northrop

Frye) have been trying to find something of the kind in the forms of literature, but the concept does not clearly provide the means for teaching students to read, write, talk, and listen well. Much more apparent is that there are various good ways of teaching English, no one of them obviously the best way, most of them suggesting that good teaching is more an art than a science. As for the aims of the English teacher, some painstaking scholar years ago made a study of the "social objectives" professed by American schools and came up with 1537 of them.

I was reminded of a study made of the presidential addresses of the American Historical Association over a period of fifty years, which revealed that the presidents disagreed on all their basic concepts and aims, agreed only that the subject of history is broad and rich. I for one would like to keep English broad and rich. I liked a metaphor used by James Britton when he suggested that English was the means of integrating all public knowledge, and learning to live. He recalled how his mother used to make jam tarts, rolling out the pastry and then cutting out a tart here, another there. "Well, we've cut out geography, we've cut out history, and we've cut out science. What do we cut out for English? I suggest we don't. I suggest that is what is left. That is the rest of it."

Only this aim of breadth immediately brings up the complexities. Many American teachers have not welcomed the guidance they are being offered by the Curriculum Study Centers. As one candidly said, "Actually, we like chaos." They prefer to go on teaching what they like most to teach, without worrying about what youngsters may need most in a given grade or will get in the next one; presumably they enjoy giving advice on telephoning and dating. Plainly some order is needed in the curriculum as a whole, some clear principle of selection in goals and materials. Yet there is as plain a danger of too much system in an age in which educationists have a rage for methodology and everything is being organized and institutionalized. While imaginative teachers may resent the system imposed on them, many others like a complete syllabus because it simplifies their problems, relieves them of all worries about what they ought to teach. Hence a reorganized program that satisfied the syllabus-lovers and examination-makers might cramp the style of independent teachers. The ideal, then, is a mean between anarchy and regimentation. It is a flexible curriculum that will bring some order out of chaos, at the same time provide some freedom of choice for teachers. But the difficult questions remain: What order? How much order? How much freedom? Not to mention the further problem of providing for the different needs of different regions, kinds of schools, kinds of students, and the individual student—the unique individual who is prized in democratic theory.

A particular complication that cropped up in every meeting of the seminar, as it will in every chapter of this book, was the differences between the American and British educational systems, traditions, and problems.[1] The participants were at first startled by their common ignorance of these differences, as well as confused now and then by differences in vocabulary. ("College students," for example, are in America students in universities, but in Britain *not* in universities.) These led to no open hostilities; the representatives of both countries were careful not to parade the superiority of their own ways, if only because they were alike dissatisfied with the state of English and intent on improving it. Each side was eager to learn from the experience of the other, the more so because there has been little direct communication between them. Both sides grew more aware

---

[1] I am including almost nothing about Canadian schools, since they were rarely mentioned in the discussions. There were only a few Canadian representatives at the seminar, and they did not dwell on any problems peculiar to their country, such as their large French-speaking population. Their schools appear to combine British and American practices, but to resemble American schools more closely.

that they were facing pretty much the same basic problems, and that their school systems, on the surface quite dissimilar, have been growing more alike in recent years. Nevertheless there remained marked differences in attitudes and approaches, some of them at first surprising.

In one of the basic papers for discussion a British writer stated: "English has no content; there are virtually no facts to transmit." Americans at once began objecting that it did have a positive content of its own, in both language and literature. Soon it appeared that to the British "content" had the disagreeable connotations of system, a set program, or a package of contents to be graded. Americans could then agree on the danger of a rigid program, but mostly they still argued for the importance of basic subject matter, the need of a definite syllabus, and the greater danger of turning a lot of mediocre teachers loose on the subject. The British typically wanted the utmost possible freedom of choice for both teachers and students. In the teaching of literature they shied away from any emphasis on "knowledge," which to them implied a body of inert facts; they deplored the tendency to present a body of historical or critical knowledge *about* literature, instead wanting to concentrate on the understanding and appreciation of particular literary works. Similarly they disliked the word "instruct," which for them connotes drilling, lecturing, or talking down. As Frank Whitehead put it, the teacher should "nudge" the young along the path of their natural development instead of instructing them in prescribed subject matter—an attitude expressed in the title of his recent book, *The Disappearing Dais.* He prefaced this book with a quotation from John Dewey, father of "progressive education."

Early in the discussions a speaker pointed to the roots of the differences on the two sides of the Atlantic. The British were reacting violently against an authoritarian tradition in schooling symbolized by stereotyped, nationwide examinations that rigidified the curriculum. They objected in particular to the "eleven-plus" examination that determined whether a youngster was admitted to a secondary school from which he might go on to a university. "On the result of a single day, a single examination, a single question, such as an English essay," wrote George Allen, "might depend your whole future and whether you became an office worker, a technician, or an artisan." Teachers have complied by simply drilling classes in the syllabus required to get them through a series of tests, and some of them into a university. Americans, on the other hand, were reacting against the slackness and confusion dating from the excesses of the progressive movement in the last generation, symbolized by the statement "We don't teach a subject, we teach the whole child." This movement broke up old habits of teaching and learning by rote, but it also encouraged a watering down of the curriculum and the introduction of the "slops" that are mistaken for English. Until the last few years schools were emphasizing "life adjustment" at the expense of intellectual content and discipline. Reformers now want students (the American word for what the British call "pupils") to be schooled more thoroughly as honest-to-God students.

Needless to add, there were wide differences of opinion within both camps. The British and Americans could also understand one another readily just because, as another speaker observed, they had passed one another in mid-Atlantic. The Americans were upholding the traditional British ideal of intellectual discipline, the British were clamoring for the individual freedom that Americans have always prized in theory; but at bottom all wanted both discipline and freedom—the best of both worlds. Still, they came at the best by different approaches. The British translated the question, "What is English?" into the operational question, "What should an English teacher do?" They answered that he should do his best to assist the development of the child; they would center the curriculum not on subject matter but on the child, his interests and immediate needs, always with an eye on individual differences. In the words of Frank Whitehead, the main business of the English teacher is not to teach the subject directly, like other subjects, but to provide "abundant opportunity for the child to use English under the conditions which will most conduce to improvement." Characteristically British schools now give much more attention than American schools to creative writing, as a means to self-discovery, self-fulfillment, self-enhancement.

Yet the two camps were never at opposite poles. As the discussions went on, with a collision of half-truths irresistible and immovable that could seem interminable, the proponents of the subject-centered and the student-centered curriculum drew closer together. The British, after all, were inevitably teaching some "content" or "knowledge"; the Americans were also much concerned about the growth of the child and the harm done by drills in lifeless knowledge. Finally the two camps arrived at a consensus in a middle ground where there were still differences of emphasis, but more significant agreements on aims. Together with the primary ability to read, write, speak, and listen well, they urged in general the need of making English a more liberal, humane study. They left it somewhat less broad than it has been in many American high schools, but considerably richer. So stated, the consensus may seem academic, not at all startling. Nevertheless, as will be seen, the recommendations of the seminar call for drastic changes in the ways English is being taught in both countries. They would require the reeducation of most teachers, principals, superintendents, school boards—and parents.

In this process of reconciliation both sides also grew more fully aware of the common problems they are up against, particularly in mass education. British secondary schools, which until recently were largely reserved for children from the upper and middle classes, have preserved an aristocratic tradition of education for the elite, with a premium on quality. The influential literary critic F. R. Leavis spoke out of this tradition when he remarked that if he had to choose between democracy and the survival of an elite, he would let democracy go. Today, however, Britain is trying to provide a good secondary school education for youngsters from the working classes too, and so is facing the problem of adapting its school system to the democratic ideal of equality that American high schools have always operated on. Some of its representatives at the seminar at times seemed to be of two minds about this novel egalitarianism (especially because they were reverent disciples of Leavis), but at the end almost all endorsed it. The American representatives accepted the democratic ideal as a matter of course, simply a basic fact of educational life. Both sides were accordingly committed to the not at all simple enterprise of maintaining quality or standards of excellence in a democratic system. And both expressed particular concern over the problem of the millions of youngsters from the city slums and semi-slums. In America this has been aggravated by the revolt of Negroes against the inferior status they have long been condemned to, but Britain too is being increasingly troubled by racial minorities as well as the many unprivileged.

The enthusiasm of reformers at the seminar was periodically dampened by reminders of another problem common to both countries—that any superior new curriculum would perforce be taught by many mediocre teachers, wedded to the old routines. In America the routines are deadlier because of the popular assumption that anybody can teach English, the language everybody knows; so about half of those who teach it in high school did not major in it in college, and the basketball coach may earn his full-time keep by giving an English class or so, even though he may be barely literate.[2] British schools have traditionally had more

---

[2] I am responsible for at least one such teacher myself, God help me: a football tackle who by dint of hard work, and prolonged hammering by

15

respect for the language, but they too are staffed with many teachers untrained for English. The seminar emphatically agreed on the need of teacher preparation programs. Whether most concerned with subject matter or with the child, all participants agreed as well on the need of smaller classes, in which students may get more individual attention. As it is, the teaching of English in both countries suffers from far too many overworked teachers in congested classrooms, bleak cells with rows of uniform desks and no facilities for imaginative projects. The brighter, better designed, better equipped schools now being built are only beginning to redeem the dreariness of the many old ones; and they too are overcrowded.

Hopes of improving the teaching of English therefore raise a vulgar economic question. Is our society willing to pay the costs? America has rushed in much more money for education in science and mathematics ever since the Russians got ahead with the first sputnik; the shortage of "scientific manpower" was called a "crisis." The country has shown no comparable concern over the state of English, or its "language manpower." For a few years the U.S. Office of Education established Project English to improve teaching, but this got much less generous support than the sciences and foreign languages. Supposedly the most fundamental subject, English is in fact commonly regarded as about the least practical one, on a par with the fine arts; congressmen do not consider it really vital to the "national interest." And what popular concern there is over it brings up deeper social problems.

For the ordinary teacher, to repeat, "good English" is simply correct English, by the standards of respectable people. Although these standards have been discredited by

---

free tutors provided by the athletic department, managed on his second try to pass Freshman Composition with a D—. This was the only English course he took in college, since his School of Physical Education provided courses more suited to his mentality.

linguists, he cannot be simply blamed for his notion because this is what he has been taught, and what his society believes. He is always under pressure to conform to the conventional beliefs of the community. In America his independence is often threatened too by organizations protesting against the teaching of "immoral," "subversive," or "un-American" books. Authors who have been banned in the schools range from Plato, Chaucer, and Thoreau to Steinbeck, Hemingway, Faulkner, and Salinger. (Shakespeare might well be added to this honor roll if patriots knew how "indecent" his Elizabethan language often is.) But it was a British teacher who first raised a question that kept recurring during the seminar. Dedicated to the development of youngsters as conscious individuals, especially by creative writing, he asked: Does our society really want such persons? Might not a slum youngster made more conscious of himself become a rebel? Might not an English teacher who helped him to discover himself be regarded as subversive? An American might add: Do the youngsters themselves really want to become conscious individuals with minds of their own? In high school they are pleased to say "Be yourself," but on questionnaires most of them say they want above all to be "well adjusted"—not clearly the best way of being oneself. Certainly most parents, as well as most personnel directors in business, want young people first of all to become well adjusted. A serious consideration of the role of English in education ultimately forces the fundamental issue of the relations of the individual and society, actual and ideal.

This issue too is matter for the chapters that follow. Here it may be said that the seminar did not conclude that the function of English teachers is to turn out rebels. Some speakers declared that the proper aims of English included the development of the child as a member of his society and inheritor of its traditional values. Others observed that ours is a pluralistic society with different sets of values, often sharply conflicting. I would emphasize the traditional belief,

17

too often disrespected in practice but at least still paid lip service, that young people ought to be trained to think honestly for themselves, and that society needs as many fully developed individuals as possible. Mark Twain's *Huckleberry Finn*—a favorite reference at the seminar with both the British and the Americans—is a case in point. Out of loyalty to his friend Jim, Huck makes his critical decision to defy conventional beliefs; he becomes a nonconformist instead of a well-adjusted boy; yet he remains the hero of a distinctively American masterpiece.

In any case the seminar agreed that teachers of literature had to be concerned with the problem of values, since writers are always dealing with them and often dramatizing conflicts of values. Obvious as this concern may seem to be, it gives English teachers another distinctive, difficult, possibly dangerous function today. Social scientists commonly say that they have no right to make value judgments, because they have no means of verifying them; and logical positivists rule them out of philosophy too for the same reason, declaring them merely subjective or emotional preferences. Nevertheless every one of us is necessarily concerned about human values, constantly forced to make judgments in everyday living as we go about trying to get the most out of life. English teachers may therefore put in a further claim for the importance of literature. It may help people to make value judgments more sensitively, in a fuller awareness of ranges of choice. Today it may oppose the notorious dehumanizing tendencies of a massive, mechanized, commercialized society. In this view the seminar also agreed tacitly that English teachers should neither impose their own personal beliefs on their students nor indoctrinate them with conventional beliefs, but rather should go out of their way to offer mature students works presenting diverse visions of life, a wide range of choices that may better enable them to decide for themselves. This seems to me an obviously fair, reasonable policy. Only the question remains whether most school boards and most parents really approve of such liberality, breadth, and richness.

Immediately, however, I would emphasize the responsibilities of the profession, especially because of its claims that English is indeed vital to the national interest and deserving of more federal support. It is a commonplace that democracy more than any other kind of society needs literate, informed, critical citizens. If it is not absolutely essential that they be able to write well, it is desirable that they be able to speak well, and certainly important that they be able to read and listen well. One way of sizing up the English curriculum—in both the schools and the colleges—is to ask how well it is serving this basic purpose, which no other subject attends to directly. Another way is to ask how well designed it is to instill a respect for, and to develop powers of discrimination in, the civilized human values that democracy attempts to make available to all its citizens. The first aim may be considered primarily a social need, the second more a need of the individual, but both are vital for a democracy in a technological age. Though they are not the only aims of a subject so broad as English, they may raise considerable question about much that goes on in the classroom, or much else that is overlooked in the curriculum.

CHAPTER TWO

DEMOCRACY IN THE CLASSROOM

The Anglo-American Seminar was most carefully planned and organized beforehand to deal one by one with all the basic problems of the teaching of English. When it assembled it was split up into a dozen groups, each with about an even representation of British and Americans, which concentrated on a particular topic and at the end reported to the seminar in a plenary session. Most of the groups were therefore troubled at first when they had some difficulty in defining and limiting their topic and realized that they were discussing the same matters as some other groups were; but eventually they got over their distress. All were of course involved in the basic question of what English is—the topic assigned one group. All had to consider their topic in relation to the broader aims of the subject; several groups submitted lists of these aims. English cannot in any case be divided up neatly into separate subjects, but the seminar was generally agreed that one trouble with it is that too often reading, writing, and speaking are taught separately, without enough attention to their intimate connections. Likewise with the group that under the title "One Road or Many?" took up the issue of what the British call "streaming" and Americans "grouping"—separating students into different classes according to their abilities. This was inextricably tied up with the problem of continuity, or the development of the child, which another party studied, while both problems showed up in the reports of still other parties. The disagreeable way of describing this state of affairs, which will be reflected in the chapters of this book, is to say that English is a messy subject. The pleasant way is to speak of the need of keeping it integrated and seeing it steadily as a whole.

The practice of streaming in England was climaxed by the "eleven-plus" examination that determined what kind of secondary school the child entered, whether a grammar school that prepared him for higher education, or one that assumed his education would end at the age of fifteen and prepared him for office or factory work. With the reorganization of the British school system after World War II, streaming spread throughout the British school system; children were separated into "A," "B," and "C" classes. The great majority of educators favored the practice, for what might seem good reason. They argued that children of different backgrounds, interests, and abilities should naturally get a different education, one suited to their needs. Teachers could soon spot the bright ones and the backward ones, those suited for the A and C tracks, and it would be unfair to hold the bright ones back in classes geared to the average. Critics of streaming were denounced as "people with left-wing sympathies," "extremists who pay homage to the ideal of equal opportunity," or simply cranks ignorant of the rudiments of education.

In the last few years, however, the critics have been

winning the day. The eleven-plus examination is on its way out; streamed secondary schools are giving way to more and more "comprehensive" ones that all kinds of students may attend. For the critics also had good reasons for their objections to streaming. At the heart of it was the social inequality that had long dominated British education, permitted few but sons of the upper classes to form their characters on the playing fields of Eton and go on to Oxford or Cambridge. Children from upper-class homes had far better opportunity to make a good showing in school than did the many more children from poor homes, especially all those condemned to slums. The glaring inequality accentuated the injustice of the eleven-plus examination, in which a child's whole future depended on the showing he made on a single day; and since the grammar schools could take only about a fifth of the children, the great majority necessarily failed. In opening the discussion of this issue, Geoffrey Summerfield pointed out a further injustice, that when children are separated into sheep and goats, most of those stigmatized as goats settle down to behaving like goats. None of the British representatives at the seminar defended streaming, at least openly.

Still, there remained some uncertainty, again for good reason. It is not social class alone that distinguishes the many gifted students from those with low IQ's. Is it reasonable and fair to put them all in the same classroom? Does this not tend to lower standards, accentuate the shortcomings of mass education? Summerfield also cited the remark of Robert Lowell that one of America's major spiritual problems was that of reconciling the claims of equality and of excellence. We are dealing with a complex issue. And it most vitally affects the teaching of English, the one subject that all youngsters are taught throughout their schooling.

America has never had such total streaming in its public schools, but as Wallace Douglas showed by a historical survey, it has come to face similar problems. The American high school began as a "common school," unstreamed, be-

25

cause it was founded to provide public education for students unable to afford the private schools. In 1894 the *Report of the Committee of Ten,* which came out of conferences attended by some hundred educators, indicated that it was still serving a common democratic purpose. The committee reported unanimous agreement that "every subject which is taught at all in secondary school should be taught in the same way and to the same extent to every pupil so long as he pursues it, no matter what the probable destination of the pupil may be, or at what point his education is to cease." English teachers said as flatly that all students—academic, technical, or terminal—should receive the same training in the mother tongue. (The committee incidentally revealed the "progress" in English by a revolutionary declaration, "that its study shall be in all respects as serious and informing as the study of Latin.") But in 1918 another famous report, *Cardinal Principles of Secondary Education,* reflected the changes that had come over the fast-growing high school. It was now being attended by "large numbers of pupils" who differed not only in "capacities" and "aptitudes" but "social heredity" and "destinies in life." While the commission that published this report still believed that the school should be treated as a model or "prototype" of society, it recognized that American society was made up of various self-conscious "groups" with special interests that had to be accommodated. Hence it recommended different curriculums for vocational purposes— "agriculture, business, clerical, industrial, fine arts, and household arts." It did not recommend streaming, since it would not commit itself to the un-American idea that this country had "classes," but it intimated some social inequality in groups that had different "social heredity" and "destinies in life."

American high schools have responded to the immense increase in the number of students since the war by offering all the variety the commission asked for, and then some. In recent years they have been making more provision for the millions of students going on to college, and with this have done more to group students according to ability. The Advanced Placement Program, for instance, is enabling superior ones to do advanced work and possibly escape the tedium of Freshman Composition in college. Such grouping differs from traditional British streaming in that it is more flexible or fluid, determined solely by interest and aptitude, and in theory involves no social inequality. Nevertheless education in America is in fact by no means free from social distinctions. Many schools are in effect streamed simply by their location; new suburban schools do much better by their students than do schools in slums. The education explosion, the sickness of the American city, and more lately the revolt of the Negroes have dramatized a problem that was long obscured by the fond illusion that all Americans were free and equal, all poor boys who worked hard could make good. Educators are now more concerned over the millions of youngsters who are politely called "disadvantaged," "underprivileged," "educationally deprived," "culturally different," "children with limited backgrounds," etc. The euphemisms may still obscure the poverty of these children, the bleak prospects indicated by a five-year-old girl who defined a wish as "something you want very bad but won't ever get." And for English teachers they are a particular problem because they naturally don't speak "good English."

On the basic issue of streaming or grouping the seminar reached a startling consensus. The mixed British-American study group unanimously condemned the practice in their report. While suggesting some provision for different interests and abilities, they asserted that the aims in teaching literature and language are fundamentally humane and should be the same for all students, at all levels. The English teacher could thus help to "overcome division between kinds of human beings," the deplorable social effects of separating and classifying youngsters. They recognized the

27

formidable obstacles, such as the many poor homes, the middle-class pressures for segregation, and the preoccupation with material values, that might make their recommendation sound like a "heavenly story with no earthly meaning"; improvement will obviously be a long, slow affair, the more difficult because it will require an overhauling of curriculums, teacher preparation, and working conditions. But this was no excuse for sitting back, only the more reason to combat vigorously the evil of "divided schools in a divided society." And in the general discussion of their report by the seminar almost all who spoke up supported it. They called for "heterogeneous" schools and classes, or in other words, for more democracy in the classroom. The prevailing sentiment was summed up in Arthur Eastman's comment that the aims of education were social as well as academic, and that not only Negroes, poor children, and the unfortunate in general suffered when they were segregated in the classroom—"We all suffer."

Yet the applause over this sentiment (which I too consider laudable) did not resolve the difficulties in theory, not to mention practice. Wallace Douglas dwelt on the reasons for doubting the principle and deploring the effects of grouping, but he concluded his paper by saying that he would not argue that it should be dropped forthwith—"though all my instincts, values, and feelings tell me to say so." The trouble is that we do not know enough about its effects, have not thought enough about the whole problem. The uncertainties become plainer as one tries to think hard. At the seminar they appeared in the comments even of some who disliked grouping.

Now, there is little or no question, I suppose, that it has bad effects on the backward and socially handicapped children, especially in a society that has made it a normal ambition to "become" somebody. Some of those who are labeled inferior may work harder to prove themselves, but most are discouraged, many may feel they are nobodies, many surely lose interest in going to school. They are likely to suffer more because most experienced teachers naturally prefer to work with the better students. Geoffrey Summerfield described a group of fifteen-year-old boys in the bottom stream or track: "They have been disapproved of, and written off, and failed, and punished, and bored, for the most part, ever since they were seven or eight years old." In America the conspicuous victims are the Negroes, most of them in schools streamed by both their poverty and their color. Long apathetic, Negro children are growing more unruly as their parents more fiercely resent their status as second-class citizens. While strengthening the argument for heterogeneous schools as a matter of simple humanity or justice, they might remind us that our schools segregate many other youngsters as backward or second-class students.

Only the trouble remains that these youngsters are in fact backward. They force the obvious question: What about the superior students? During the chorus of attacks on grouping, one participant asked: Did they really disapprove of the common practice of putting these students in special classes? Another asked: Did Americans want to abolish the Advanced Placement Program that was encouraging high schools to provide advanced study for students capable of it? An Englishman to whom I expressed some surprise over the apparent unanimity of his compatriots on this issue suggested privately, and a little bitterly, that I ask them what kind of schools they sent their own children too; like it or not, the grammar schools are reputed to have distinctly higher standards than the comprehensive ones. An American expressed publicly his unhappiness over a once distinguished high school in his home city that was now 90 percent Negro and much deteriorated. Hard-core white liberals were still sending their sons and daughters to this school, but he was not: he was unwilling to sacrifice their education, make them pay for his democratic principles. Parents can hardly be blamed for wanting the best possible education for their children, with special opportunities and incentives for the abler ones.

The answers to such objections need not rest on democratic sentiment alone. The study group reported some evidence that grouping had only a slight effect on the abler students, while a bad effect on the much larger middle range of students. But perhaps the best case for mixed classes is the advantage of variety. Youngsters from different backgrounds, with different interests and aptitudes, may not only learn to get along better, as people have to in a democratic society, but may stimulate one another. English classes in particular may be livelier because of the diverse experience they bring to their reading and writing. The less able students are not uniformly duller than the bright ones; they may have more aptitude for some purposes, write or talk more imaginatively. English likewise best illustrates another objection to grouping: the stress on examinations that it encourages. The criteria by which students are judged and tracked are always somewhat uncertain, beginning with "intelligence," which cannot be measured precisely, or for that matter precisely defined; but skills and aptitudes in reading and writing are harder to measure than knowledge or ability in other subjects. It is dangerous to label a child as positively incapable of good work in English; British teachers reported some impressive results they had got with children of low IQ's, the "rejected." And the bright children too may suffer from the pressures of examinations, becoming more interested in getting good grades than in getting a good education, pursuing their interests independently. They may think of English as something that needs only to be passed and then dropped for good.

Again, however, the uncertainties are indicated by the "may" in these statements. Children from upper and lower classes do not necessarily learn to get along better when thrown together; often they do not want to mix, and the outcome may be a sharper antagonism, as too many Negro children are learning. Bright children may be stimulated by variety, or they may be bored by the pace of classes geared to the average. We can never be sure that they will do as well in mixed classes. We can be sure that they can advance faster in classes designed for them and that too many have been held back by the average. Nor is grouping simply undemocratic or inhumane, any more than is a concern for standards of excellence beyond the capacity of most students. It may be more humane to relieve backward students of direct competition with superior ones, which may give them more pronounced feelings of inferiority than placement in classes suited to their needs. American high schools in particular are heterogeneous, even in suburbia, and are never two-track affairs, with a complete separation of sheep and goats. I doubt that many American youngsters feel humiliated by being labeled as mediocre in English (especially if they are good at athletics or popular socially), but in any case they may do as well as good English students in mathematics or other subjects. The high schools offer options that help goats to feel like sheep in some courses, and they offer as well a wide variety in respectable vocational training.

They also bring up another complication. The case against grouping is strongest in the early grades, where except for remedial work it is least common; most children can grasp the rudiments. As they go on and do more advanced work, however, differences in capacity become more pronounced and more of a problem in mixed classes. By the last years of high school some students can enjoy literature that is far over the heads of others; some have a fluency that makes more painful the laborious efforts of others to write passably. If such inequalities are due in part to faulty schooling, they have in any case to be reckoned with and make it harder to maintain equality, not to mention high standards. And with the approach of higher education, the most serious problem becomes the persistence of the democratic fallacy— the popular notion that all middle-class Americans are properly entitled to such an education whether or not they have the intellectual capacity for it.[1]

The best answer the study group proposed to all such objections was the British "workshop" method, which may be combined with recent American experiments in team teaching. The objections to heterogeneous classes arise primarily because they are in effect often homogenized classes, usually too large, of which an English teacher may have five a day; it is impossible for the teacher to give individual attention to so many diverse students. In the workshop the class is split up into a number of groups of varied interests or aptitudes, perhaps self-chosen, which work together under the guidance of the teacher; each group may then be given a different assignment related to some larger project, such as making up a magazine. One example offered was a British teacher's work with a mixed class in a school in a slum-clearance district, where the average IQ was below one hundred. He split up his classes into "crews" of trawlers, each with a captain, which dipped into a pot for instructions where to sail and at what speed, and day by day for further information about winds, storms, their catch, when to return, etc. They made a large map of the North Sea on which they marked their positions with model boats they made; they kept a log and sent wireless messages back to port; they calculated the value of their catch by current prices, and then their wages; they listened to sea music, such as Debussy's *La Mer;* they wrote descriptions of the storm, sea chanties, and accounts of their activities. At the end they made a trip to Hull and visited the docks. So the youngsters worked eagerly together, each contributing according to his

---

[1] I have heard a top administrator in a state university complain to a faculty group that too many students were being failed. It was bad publicity, he pointed out, souring taxpayers and legislators on the university, but it was also undemocratic: if students couldn't pass the university's courses, then it should design courses they could pass. He neglected to add that schools of physical education do precisely this for many hired athletes who give the university good publicity.

interests and ability, while learning something about quite a few subjects.

Such imaginative teaching cannot be carried on in an ordinary classroom with its rows of desks. It requires materials and facilities not usually available to teachers—one thing the study group had in mind when it called for better working conditions. Other groups joined it in requesting more and better facilities for teaching English—classrooms with movable furniture, space for drama work, some books other than textbooks, and such equipment as film and strip projectors, screens, sound recording booths, and tape recorders. That English teachers have had to get along with nothing but books and blackboards is no reason why they should not have special facilities such as teachers of science and other technical subjects always have. But this raises the recurrent question. Do school boards, parents, and taxpayers consider English "practical" enough to warrant the additional expense? More broadly, is our society willing to pay for the many new schools needed to give more attention to the individual it prizes in theory?

Meanwhile the issue of grouping remains unsettled. It seems to me clearly undesirable to do away with all grouping under present conditions. It also seems to me clearly possible to do much more to realize the advantages of variety in mixed public schools. At least the spirit of the seminar's report was admirable. If the group evaded some of the complexities, it avoided as well the simplification implicit in its assigned subject, "One Road or Many?" It did not come out for one road in the sense of a single curriculum for all students, nor did it agree with the *Report of the Committee of Ten* that every subject "should be taught in the same way and to the same extent to every pupil." Essentially it agreed with Geoffrey Summerfield's conclusion: not one way *or* many but one way *and* many—"a system, that is, that respects both equalities and inequalities." Schools might experiment with various systems.

33

In this spirit I take up a final complication of the issue of democracy in the classroom—that individual prized in democratic theory, about whom the British representatives especially were so much concerned. He entered the discussion in ways that were often not explicit. Those who opposed streaming or grouping dwelt mostly on the injustice to all the "disadvantaged" children, which among other things meant that they were given little chance to realize and develop their individuality, to be or become persons in their own right. Those who doubted that all grouping should be done away with were thinking of the superior students, gifted individuals whose development might be hindered. Behind their differences lay the agreement that the issue of grouping was especially important in the teaching of English, not merely because this went on in every school grade, but because its humane aims included more than impersonal knowledge or practical skills; mastery of language and appreciation of literature contribute more directly to the development of personality than do other major subjects in the curriculum. And behind all discussion lay the issue of the actual and the ideal relation of the individual to society in modern democracy.

One of the British representatives, Glyn Lewis, tried most persistently to moderate and supplement the tendencies of his compatriots to stress chiefly individual differences, the intimate or unique rather than the public, and the teacher's duty merely to "nudge" the child along the path of his personal development. He pointed out that with all due respect to the child, society has its claims too; its nature and needs must be considered. It properly seeks to inculcate its values, secure his loyalty, and promote national unity, to which the study of language and literature can contribute much. The child himself needs not only adventure but security. He needs the feeling of shared experience and the sense of belonging to his society, sharing in its cultural heritage. It follows that streaming by class is bad in a democratic society, since it threatens both unity and the security of the lowly, creates in them a feeling of not belonging. But grouping by interest and ability may be helpful in meeting the demands of a heterogeneous society; homogeneous groups within mixed schools can promote stability and security. Briefly, Lewis sought to maintain a principle of balance in the personal development of youngsters, between their varying needs as individuals and their common needs as members of a society.

To this one might say that society today needs no help in taking care of itself. Its ruling values are constantly inculcated, not only in most homes, schools, and churches but by the mass media and all the organs of business. Long ago De Tocqueville, Emerson, John Stuart Mill, and others began worrying about the exceptional power that a democracy has over its members. It is not political but social power, the power of public opinion—the pressures to which school teachers are always subjected. It is the tyranny of the majority generated by the principle of equality: the tyranny of the "common man" who distrusts unconventional thought, the uncommon man, the egghead, and resents efforts to hold him up to standards of excellence or criticism of his paltry pleasures. Today—to cut short a too familiar story—these tendencies are magnified by high-powered, low-geared industries selling the values of conformity and mediocrity. Hence the plainest need in education today is to maintain other values that were fostered by the democratic principle of equality—the right of every person to have a mind and a life of his own, and the value of realizing his individuality. As for the study of literature, it may promote national unity, but it is more clearly helpful in the development of personality and of respect for quality.

In this regard the seminar's report on grouping approached an ideal balance. If it gave too little thought to superior students, it emphasized what I think people most need to realize, the injustice being done to millions of handicapped children. For the rest it was trying to respect the rights and the needs of all children, both as unique individuals and as human beings with much in common. Its stated objective was by no means to level down or lower standards, but to educate all to the best of their capacities. In the workshop it presented a model of a democratic classroom, with students of different interests and abilities cooperating instead of merely competing, in groups that fostered not mere groupism or togetherness but industry and self-reliance in a common endeavor, and under the guidance of a teacher who stimulated and collaborated but did not simply instruct, prescribe, or lay down the law. And if this heavenly story has too little earthly meaning for most teachers in schools as they are today, there is something to be said for setting sights high. One speaker commented that a dream program may help more than practical tinkering by both inspiring and guiding effort toward ideal objectives.

CHAPTER THREE

THE DEVELOPMENT OF THE CHILD

Nothing is plainer than that the English curriculum should have some kind of continuous, cumulative development from the first grade to the end of high school, corresponding to the simple fact that children keep growing up. If one asks, however, what is the order of this continuity and what its guiding principle, one finds the usual state: a vast curricular disorder and no clear principle. The study group that focused on this problem at once ran into the basic differences between the two delegations, the British inclining to look for the principle of order in the psychological development of the child, the Americans looking more to subject matter or objective principles of knowledge. At the end, the seminar did not come out with either a definite order or a principle definite enough to provide one. The consensus seemed to be that we had to have more continuity, that we do not know just how to plan it, and that we should never impose any definite program on all students alike.

Nevertheless I was again neither surprised nor dismayed by this outcome. Since I wearied at times of the continual clashing of half-truths, I was gratified by the eventual success of the seminar in not only clarifying but resolving many of its differences, and arriving at a measure of consensus that again involved a positive rejection of much current practice in the schools. The study group agreed to accept the development of the child as its working principle. Americans could appreciate that this helped to keep English humane and alive, while allowing them to continue stressing the need of appropriate subject matter. The British preference for focusing on the personal and the inner life, helping the child to order, extend, and enrich his experience instead of imparting a body of knowledge or mere techniques, still required attention to his knowing and knowing how as well as his feelings. The differences in emphasis or approach served to alert both sides to the risks and the possible excesses of their approach, and so finally enabled them to reach more agreement. And the consensus was closest on a subject in which a difference of vocabulary at first caused some misunderstanding—the young child.

The British mean by "child" the youngster to the age of fifteen, the end of his compulsory education. (By 1970 this is to be extended to sixteen.) Americans think of the child as a grade school youngster and more sharply distinguish him from the high school student, who by graduation is a young man. Their representatives were especially interested in the problems of teaching English in the high schools, since these are now preparing most of their students for college—a far greater proportion than move on in Britain. The British remained more interested in younger students, who got much more attention at the seminar than did advanced ones. But the possibly disproportionate attention given to the little ones (of whom I also wearied at times)

can be justified by the great importance of the early forma-
tive years, and especially by the misfortune that their
natural lively interest in reading, writing, and talking in
class is too often killed in grade school. A particular problem
of English teachers is how not only to develop but simply to
preserve this natural interest as the child grows up.

Most people do not realize an elementary truth that
was repeatedly brought up at the seminar. The child mas-
ters the basic structure of his language by the age of five,
before he enters school. What this means may be illustrated
by my own belated realization of this truth years after I
started teaching, when I helped a Mexican schoolmaster
who was trying to learn English. "Want you to go to town
with me?" he asked one day, showing off the progress he
was making. For the first time I became aware how we used
"do" to ask questions, and I improvised a rule to this effect.
The next day the schoolmaster asked as proudly, "Do you
be my friend?" I then had to explain that the verb "to be"
was an exception to the rule, and after a moment's thinking
added that it was the only exception, hoping I was right.
(I wasn't.) An English-speaking five-year-old unconsciously
knows these and many other rules. With all this grammar
he has picked up a vocabulary of several thousand words,
including a great deal of idiom that troubles foreigners. He
will soon know, if he doesn't already, that one arrives *at* five
o'clock, *on* Wednesday, *in* May, or just next week, without
a preposition—a word he has never heard of. Altogether,
the child's mastery of language is a marvelous feat considering how elaborate and intricate a system language is; it has
been described as "the greatest intellectual achievement any
of us ever makes." In a second of talking the child obeys
five or six rules, and he makes only about one mistake in
ten seconds.

Then the trouble begins. The teacher may seize on that
mistake, beginning to shatter the child's confidence without
realizing how much he has mastered by himself. As the

child goes on in school the problem becomes more difficult. He *has* to grow more conscious of his language, learn much more about how to use it. But need he be conscious of all the rules that teachers usually try to drill into him?

The seminar was much impressed by a consultant, Sybil Marshall, who has taught children in England. She protested against the traditional discipline that has called for silence in the classroom and premature emphasis on mistakes. She dwelt on the rich possibilities in the child's own exploration of language, his interest in words, his pleasure in using more of them. To illustrate she told of a child who was stamping around the room strumming on a toy guitar like a Beatle, singing a lyric of his own composing—"Maximum capacity, maximum capacity!" The teacher's job is to supply the children plentifully with stories, poems, jingles, songs, and pictures, let them begin selecting for themselves, create an atmosphere of freedom and pleasure in which they continually use words, and take care neither to separate reading, writing, and talking nor to isolate English from other arts. Mrs. Marshall goes so far as to say that she would ban exercises in grammar, punctuation, and spelling. In *Experiment in Education* (1963) she wrote:

> I would give them enough patterns, but not in the form of exercises. I would give them patterns in speech, in books, in poetry, and in plays. I would not subject my pupils to ten minutes a day under the ultraviolet lamp of intense grammatical exercises, but would instead seek out every patch of literary sunshine and see to it that the pupils worked and played in its warmth and light until grammatical usage and good style, the balance and cadence of sentences, and the happy choice of the most significant words soaked into them through every one of their senses. . . . It is much more important, surely, to be bursting with things to write about and not know precisely how to write them, than to know all the rules and not have anything to write.

Such methods smack of the old progressive education in America, now in disrepute, and may recall the cartoon of the child asking the teacher one morning: "Must we do what we want to do today?" To the seminar Mrs. Marshall's way of teaching nevertheless seemed admirable; if some members had reservations, no one stood up to defend the traditional discipline and all the exercises that go with it. I should say that what she teaches (and from all accounts with brilliant success) is by no means mere pastime or "life adjustment." It is strictly English—the fundamentals of reading, writing, talking, and listening, learning to use language better. It pays sufficient respect to subject matter as well as to the growing child. Sooner or later there has to be attention to mistakes (a matter that the British tended to introduce as an afterthought or polite concession), but on the face of the school record constant drilling in exercises is hardly a successful way of eliminating mistakes in writing and speaking. The record makes much plainer that in the later grades many long-drilled youngsters no longer like to write, and themselves say that they have nothing to write about. They may be deaf to the lilt of "maximum capacity." In America they will soon think that poetry is an unnatural form of writing, pleasure in it is natural only to girls.

Miriam Wilt, an American specialist in the teaching of young children, brought out the larger implications of this issue by deploring the extreme revulsion against progressive education. She noted that the Russian sputnik that caught the defense establishment off guard called out a search for scapegoats and cries for a return to the three R's. "Before long scientists or mathematicians who didn't know a six-year-old human child from a rhesus monkey were telling teachers not only what to teach but how to teach." Actually progressive education in its heyday had little effect on most schools; they remained too much like the schools early in the century. Change was generally slow and cautious, and much of it was by common consent for the better. Among its by-products was the child study movement that became influential in the forties. Even the talk about teaching "the whole child" instead of merely a subject made sense when the subject was reading and writing. I would add the guess that John Dewey, who has been made the No. 1 scapegoat by the educational FBI's, had much less to do with the current stress on life adjustment and social activities than has the rise of the teenager. The seminar might have paid more attention to this teenager, historically a quite novel type, who has come with the affluent society, and whose interests are catered to by an immense entertainment and service industry as well as the schools.

None of the American representatives at the seminar, at any rate, flatly repudiated the aims and methods of the progressive education movement. Most accepted more readily the British view of the centrality of the child because they did not hold out for the old ways of teaching the three R's, and they wanted the child to learn by actively participating instead of merely listening, reciting, and repeating. At the same time, the British representatives heeded the American warnings about the "disaster" that overtook progressive education. They took more pains to make clear that the freedom they wanted for children was not the license of fancy or self-indulgence, but a way of stimulating them to use their own heads and work more wholeheartedly. One of the warmest advocates of such freedom concluded in a final statement that "above all we need an easy, though *not* easy-going, civilized atmosphere in the classroom." A report approved by a mixed group veered a little further to the left in declaring that the classroom should provide "a relatively permissive atmosphere, free from heavy adult censoriousness," and that criticism of a student's talk or composition "must be introduced very delicately," subordinated to his right to expect from his audience first of all "*a reply to what he has said.*"

On the teaching of young children, in short, the semi-

nar appeared to be substantially agreed. The problem remained that children keep growing up. In the first grades
the teacher's chief need is to know the child, since the subject matter is rudimentary and diffuse; penmanship, reading,
writing, and the like take up about half the day. Later English becomes a single subject, taught in a single period, and
subject matter raises harder questions. The seminar did not
agree—or even try to agree—on just what and how the
youngsters should be taught in successive grades. And let
me add at once that I see no possible means of agreement—
just because English is more intimately involved in their
development than is any other subject and ideally can do
most to assist it.

Specific problems in the teaching of literature and composition will be considered in later chapters. Here our concern is the underlying problems of children's development
as a whole. To begin with, this development may seem clear
enough in its broad outlines (if only because the child grows
up), but it may be described in various ways. In a lecture on
"The Rhythm of Education," the philosopher Alfred North
Whitehead made out three main stages of growth: the stage
of romance or first apprehension, when subject matter has
the vividness of novelty for the child; the stage of precision,
comprising the period of secondary education; and the stage
of generalization, marking the entrance into manhood. Frank
Whitehead offered teachers somewhat more specific clues in
a paper that served as the basis for discussion of continuity.
The growing child naturally acquires a larger vocabulary
and some control over more complex sentence structures,
but also more awareness of different audiences and situations and some ability to adapt his writing and talking to
different purposes; he grows more capable of handling ab-
stractions, sorting his experience into categories, and going
beyond the concrete here and now to symbolic thinking; he
grows more discriminating, capable of critical judgments of
both what he reads and what he writes; in literature he

moves from fantasy and wish fulfillment to something more complex and impersonal; and so on.

All this leaves open, however, the question how much he is capable of at any given stage, what materials he should be given, what the teacher should do to assist his growth—not to mention how to meet complaints of parents that Johnnie is being asked to read things too hard for him, or maybe too childish for him. James Moffett made a heroic effort to be more systematic in a paper "Toward a Model of Continuity," suggesting the model building that is now the fashion in the social sciences. He offered a grid chart, with curves and arrows, to represent parallels between stages of growth in ways of thinking and ways of speaking: in thought, coordinating objects and events, inducing categories, relating categories to form propositions, and deriving implications by combining propositions; and in speech or writing, narrative, exposition, explanation and generalization, and theory, or "statements about statements." This chart satisfied nobody, including its author. Moffett described it as a model "arrested in mid-agony," adding that he was afraid some publisher might leap at it. I mention it chiefly to illustrate my belief that model building is not going to help much in this problem of teaching English, but that it is too likely to become fashionable among educationists, if it is not already.

A constant complaint in the discussions of the problem was that we do not know enough about the development of children; we need much more research. Teaching in the early grades has been assisted by the pioneering work of child psychologists, such as the studies of Piaget, whom the British often referred to.[1] Psychologists have done much less work on older children. Linguists at the seminar called for

---

[1] I believe Piaget's books are highly esteemed in America too, but are not so well known to the general public as they ought to be. Here I would recommend in particular *The Thought and Language of the Child*. See also John H. Flavell, *The Developmental Psychology of Jean Piaget* (1963).

more cooperation with them and with social scientists in research on development, but they also warned that it is an
infant discipline, which is turning out much dubious material; the trouble is that half-baked ideas are always likely
to get frozen in textbooks and institutionalized prematurely.
My impression remains that this is the chief trouble since
educators have come to be called education*ists*.

An example of particular concern here is some uncertainty over the pace of the child's development. The consensus at the seminar seemed warmest when Wayne Booth,
an American advocate of the formal rhetoric that the British
were cool to, said that the fourth grade should not be taught
for the sake of the fifth grade, every assignment should be
its own reward, and no child should be pushed into con-
ceptualizing until he has reached a level of operations where
he wants to do so for its own sake. On the latter point, Frank
Whitehead wrote that "such premature 'forcing' is one of
the most prevalent causes of backwardness and apathy."
My impression, however, is that the tendency in American
schools is in general not to force children enough, and that
in a country too much inclined to make everything easy the
chief need is to guard against underrating their abilities,
keep them more on the stretch. This was partially confirmed
by a recent study made by Ruth Strickland, which indicated
that children are well ahead of their school readers, up to a
more mature style. The editors of the best-selling *World
Book Encyclopedia,* designed for youngsters, nevertheless
operate on the assumption that a twelve-year-old is capable
of grasping only short, simple sentences and would be
floored by a semicolon. They claim the authority of an edu-
cationist who has conducted research on this matter and who
maintains that high school students also want or need this
childish style—a belief that might be supported by the example of editorial writers in the tabloids. Since it appears that
one can appeal to some research findings to back up almost
any tactic, I assume that authors of textbooks and manuals

will be disposed to play it safe, and when in doubt choose to make things easy or agreeable.

A broader problem that can hardly be settled by any research is the practical necessity of considering not only the psychological development of the child but the needs of society, and his own practical, social needs, reflecting the culture that affects his development. In America the social and the intellectual aims of education are too often confused, so that much extraneous material is included in the English curriculum; yet these aims cannot be sharply separated either—and certainly not by a seminar that made so much of the social injustice of streaming or grouping. One study group recommended that students be given some training in writing business letters and even a bit of casual advice about the uses of the telephone. Such concessions to impurity bring up larger questions. How much, for example, should the English curriculum be modified to fit the interests and needs of students headed for business or industry, not college? Or if not at all, on the assumption that the primary concern is always the psychological development of the youngster, how much attention should be given to the special interests and problems of adolescents in selecting materials and topics? Those who wish to think primarily in terms of intellectual development have to face still another complication. At best the curve of development is rough, never precise enough to permit certainty in selection of appropriate material or decision on priorities in skills, but it is never uniform either; children plainly develop at different rates, because of which some are called slow or backward. In the broad agreement of the seminar that these children should nevertheless be included in mixed classes, the objection that they would not be up to literature suited to the superior students was met by the answer that the teacher should give them different books to read, within their capacity. The implication, it would seem, is that some special provision might be made for technical students, adolescents, or any other common type.

Now, such difficulties in designing a cumulative curriculum seem to me no reason for anguish or despair. Teachers of a subject so broad as English, and so vitally related to the growth of young people, can keep it "pure" only by an academic exclusiveness. The surest guide through the uncertainties about what they should teach is not scientific method but humanistic principles of breadth, balance, and flexibility. I have mentioned a few difficulties because they may help one to take a calmer view of the deeper differences between the British and the Americans on the problems of continuity, and to understand better the kind of agreement they reached even though the differences could never be completely resolved.

Throughout the discussions of the problem, and of the specific problems taken up in the following chapters, most of the British continued to shy away from stress on "knowledge" or "content," a body of facts to be learned about language and literature. They looked somewhat askance at "skills" too, stress on practical techniques rather than language as a means of exploring, illuminating, ordering, and shaping personal experience. (Frank Whitehead noted a deep significance in the observation of E. M. Forster: "How can I know what I think till I hear what I say?") Keeping in mind the young child and his unconscious mastery of language, they soft-pedaled the teaching of rules, principles, forms, and all such external aids; the important thing is that the student be able to read and write well, whether or not he is conscious of all the means of doing so. Similarly they tended to minimize his need of a critical vocabulary and formal knowledge in developing critical ability, at least until he is quite advanced; they argued that children are usually asked to verbalize and conceptualize before they have had enough working experience to give them an "internalized" understanding. As for the role of the teacher, the British remained fearful of the idea of his "instructing" youngsters, and continue to talk of nudging them along, guiding them, obliquely directing them, but taking care not to "intervene" in their natural, rightful development.

On all these matters most of the Americans took a more conventional stand. Emphasizing the necessity of knowledge for proficiency or real mastery, they inclined to retain more systematic teaching of subject matter and to stress more the value of a conscious understanding of forms and principles, as in all other disciplines. They dwelt on the claims of the subject as well as the child, alike in the study of language, rhetoric, and literature. Less fearful of "instruction," they may have shared my own unspoken sentiment. While appreciating the concern of the British for the tender minds of youngsters, I felt there was some need of asserting the rights of teachers too, or even their duty to "intervene" now and then when their mature judgment of a child's needs differed from his. Children are not defenseless, after all; and especially with older ones in America the most apparent need seems to me more discipline, more respect for authority. (As a parent I have been disposed to resent a popular remark of teenagers to their elders: "That's what *you* think.")

Nevertheless both sides could agree to disagree because the basic difference between them was only one of emphasis or degree, never a matter of knowledge *versus* proficiency, never a simple either-or. Both recognized that we could not be sure just how much explicit knowledge students needed to acquire the proficiency they agreed was more important, or just when and to what extent youngsters should be introduced to formal concepts and asked to put into words what they were learning about reading and writing and judging. In particular both agreed that there is a great deal of dead wood in the English curriculum today. In the name of a "no-nonsense" policy, schools require students to learn too much *about* English, give too much routine instruction in knowledge that has little live meaning for them. For the popular idea that an educated person is one who knows a lot is congenial to most teachers too. External knowledge is the easiest thing to teach, and to test on examinations.

With advanced students, however, differences in policy remained marked. They sprang from a fundamental difference between the school systems of the two countries. Secondary education in Britain ends with the sixth form, attended by students from the age of roughly sixteen to eighteen, which carries them considerably further than American high schools do in preparing students for college. When admitted to a university, its graduates do not have to take Freshman English, since they have demonstrated sufficient proficiency in English, and if they specialize in the subject, they can be trusted to have an extensive knowledge of literature. The British representatives complained chiefly of the standardized curriculum of the sixth form, which has been largely fixed by external examinations that determine admission to universities; these have put a premium on ability to write expository and literary essays and on knowledge about literature. The American complaint, on the other hand, was that curriculums in high schools are so varied and formless that college teachers cannot count on their students having had an adequate training in either language or literature; many may know almost nothing about anything written before 1900. The Curriculum Study Centers have therefore been busy designing programs with sequences, extending from the last years of grade school through high school, which will assure a sounder, more comprehensive training. The British showed little interest in these programs except worry over the very idea of a program—it smacked of the fixed syllabus they want to get rid of. They found it hard to realize that American college teachers can never take for granted even the limited acquaintance with the literary classics that they did.

The work of these study centers was barely mentioned by the study group that reported on the problems of continuity, or in the general discussion of its report. There was some excuse for this neglect, apart from the concentration on the development of the little tots. The centers have issued many volumes of diverse materials, which nobody had time to study at the crowded seminar. I cannot myself pretend to have explored these volumes, much less read them all. But from looking through a number of them I got pretty much the impression summed up by Alfred Kitzhaber, himself director of the Oregon Curriculum Study Center for the last four years. In opening the seminar he said:

> I would like to be able to tell you that they have all been carefully planned, and that each has been assigned to work on a predetermined segment or aspect of the curriculum to insure uniform coverage of the whole. I would like to assure you that the work of all two dozen is being carefully coordinated, and that all are producing uniformly excellent results. None of these is true. We are all muddling along, working hard but often rather aimlessly, sometimes producing new and exciting materials, sometimes just warming up the old and serving them under a new name.

Kitzhaber then pointed to the familiar root trouble: "We have no generally accepted philosophy of our subject to build upon, one that defines and orders it, one that has been scrutinized by the best minds that can be brought to bear upon it and has their endorsement." Many of the most important questions have not been answered; some may not even have been asked. So we are back where we started: What is English?

We are not, however, all at sea. Kitzhaber also added that excellent materials were coming out of the study centers; some courses that might have only the charm of novelty were still to the good in a subject so hagridden by obsolete tradition as English, and most of the new courses were an improvement on the old ones—all of which implies that we do have acceptable standards of judgment. Other Americans working at the study centers assured the British that there was no danger of their imposing a uniform syllabus on the schools. The new courses were serving merely as guides and at that were not simply thrust at teachers by outsiders; teachers were collaborating in designing them. Many teachers who at first either balked at them or swallowed them whole were now showing more discrimination, getting and enjoying more freedom of choice. George Allen of England, who had visited a number of American universities and schools on behalf of the United Kingdom Department of Education, reported his impression that any theoretical danger of a uniform syllabus was minimal because the study centers were offering teachers a greater variety of material and many more possibilities of individual choice than most had enjoyed before. He warned chiefly against the danger of oversimplifying the whole problem, regarding Americans as ruthless disciplinarians suppressing the child, the British as eccentric individualists thinking only of the child.

At least the seminar agreed unanimously that there should never be a uniform syllabus or fixed program. On the problems of continuity it therefore again agreed in effect that there is no one road, but many. No one tried to define the "natural" sequence of English studies from the beginning of school to the end because there is no such thing. We can make out roughly stages in the child's development, because of which we can all agree that he should begin with nursery rhymes and fairy tales before *Hamlet*, but there is no way of deciding just when it is best for him to read *Hamlet* or how much he should be expected to know and say about it. Similarly we know that he needs to enlarge his vocabulary and will do so haphazardly and unconsciously by himself, but no teacher who wants to help him systematically can know just what words he needs to know next. Having dwelt on a number of troublesome questions, I should finally say simply that there is not only no possibility but no need of positive, conclusive answers. For informed teachers experience can be a sufficient guide. The seminar contributed chiefly by sharpening awareness of the problems, making clearer the need of tact and flexibility, and agreeing upon the aim of providing more diverse and abundant opportunity for development through the uses of language.

Or if this seems too simple, let me end with some of the inevitable complications. The materials that the Curriculum Study Centers are adding to the immense wealth of materials, already available in textbooks are not simply a boon; they complicate the problem of selection and may confirm the addiction to packaged materials. Some of the new courses are warmed up versions of old ones just because teachers are collaborating; many teachers naturally tend to prefer familiar routines, want only the appearance of novelty. The many separate packets for language study, composition, and literature accentuate a tendency to specialization that splits English up into separate subjects. While the seminar agreed that reading, writing, and speaking should not be sharply separated, as they too often are in the later grades, keeping them integrated becomes ever harder in advanced courses. A study group that took up this problem could not agree on a solution. Some thought unity and coherence could be best secured by having one teacher in charge of the class; others thought that since most teachers lack some of the necessary skills, specialists would be needed to help out. In either case, more depends upon the teacher in English than in other major subjects, especially when it is agreed that he should do more than teach a body of knowledge or mere techniques. Designers of new curriculums in English cannot bank on the hope of "teacher-proof" materials that inspires some enthusiasts in the new mathematics and new science.

CHAPTER FOUR

"GOOD ENGLISH"

Since language is the medium of all education, it might seem that no subject is more fundamental than linguistics, the systematic study of the nature, structure, and history of language. Actually the seminar displayed mixed feelings about the subject. The linguists in its midst were kept unhappily aware that some of the British viewed their study with a suspicion verging on animosity—worrying as usual over the possible reduction of English to "knowledge" and "content." Nevertheless there was virtually unanimous agreement on the value of their contributions to an understanding of usage. To my mind, nothing said at the seminar was more important for the general public to hear about than what the linguists had to say in their final report.

As they pointed out, language is necessarily involved in everything that English teachers teach—it can never be separated from composition or literature. Plainly, then, teachers ought to have a proper understanding of their language. In fact most of them do not. They are still carrying around and passing on discredited, false notions about "correct" English. Their misunderstanding of the structure and the operation of language is more dangerous because they are sure of the correctness of their notions, ignorant of their ignorance; their whole attitude toward language needs to be changed. And so with most parents, the educated public; they may admit to limited knowledge, but they too tend to be most confident about their erroneous notions. None of the British objected to the conclusion of the linguists: "No education can be adequate in which knowledge of our native language, knowledge of the mother tongue, is false, or shallow, or trivial." And the problem here is more serious because it is not merely educational but social, involving deep-seated prejudices that tend to thwart democracy in the schools and stunt the development of children.

The immediate problem centers on Standard English, or what is popularly known as "good English." As defined by the linguists, this is a dialect that originated in the region of London some five or six centuries ago and has since spread, with variations, all over the English-speaking world. It is the English used by educated people when carrying on their affairs publicly. It is therefore the language of not only literature and learning but also church and school, government and law, all the professions. It is so familiar that in a sense it is easy to recognize—the reader is reading it right now. Yet there is no single, fixed, "right" form of Standard English. It embraces many forms, varying with country, profession, and purpose. In particular it has two distinct major varieties, written and spoken English. It is always fluid, growing and changing with usage, which determines correctness. And though as the language of the educated and the ruling classes it is a "prestige dialect," well for all the ambitious to master, it is not necessarily, intrinsically superior in all respects to other dialects. Often it borrows from them, in time making many a slang expression respectable English.

The popular idea of it, however, is quite different. To most people its chief distinction is correctness, and correctness is supposedly determined by a fixed, uniform, permanent standard, comparable in authority to the Ten Commandments.[1] The standard is set by the dictionary, whose editors are regarded as legislators of language when not dictators. This notion produced the recent furore over Webster's Third *New International Dictionary*, which admitted much common usage that had not been considered respectable. English professors led the attacks on its policy as "an outrage" or "a very great calamity." In a commencement address one orated that such failures to maintain standards of good English were sins against our whole heritage, even crimes against humanity.

In the schools misconceptions of Standard English have produced "schoolmarm English," taught as if it were a dead language, like Latin. In particular teachers have treated spoken English as simply an inferior form of written English, instead of a properly different form, and assumed that "colloquial" means corrupt. They have taught their students never to write in the natural ways they talked; they have even tried to make them talk more in the way they were supposed to write. Likewise they have "corrected" much natural pronunciation, teaching that *interesting*, for example, must have four syllables. The one thing that youngsters were sure to learn was that classroom English is quite different from normal speech. In class you recited "I shall leave" when conjugating, as if you had never heard of "I'm going to leave." I have found that college freshmen who were almost

---

[1] In America the obsession with correctness has incidentally made a fetish of spelling as a major requirement of good writing. Of the 1537 "social objectives" of schools that were dug up by the scholar I mentioned earlier, the most popular was correct spelling.

illiterate could always be trusted to know one rule—never end a sentence with a preposition. It is pleasant to recall Winston Churchill's comment: "This is the kind of pedantry up with which I will not put."

Still, the issue here is not simple. At the seminar there were signs of excessive nervousness over pedantry: in various statements of the aims of English no one dared to include speaking and writing "correctly"—it was always "appropriately," "effectively," etc. Granted that usage obviously decides what is acceptable, as Horace said two thousand years ago, there remains the obvious need of maintaining standards. Americans in particular have an ambiguous attitude towards English, on the one hand supporting the mania for correctness in the schools, on the other being notoriously careless in their speech habits. Sloppy usage is no less sloppy for being standard with a hundred million Americans (including such eminent ones as ex-President Eisenhower). One who respects the language may deplore accepted confusions like *disinterested* with *uninterested, infer* with *imply,* which blur the meanings of words and clutter up the language with more needless synonyms. In our slack, complacent society one may argue that the real problem is not so much schoolmarm English as lazy English.

Albert Marckwardt presented a judiciously balanced statement of the issue in an introductory paper on standards and attitudes. He granted that when the linguists started crusading years ago they had too much fun kicking over ash cans, slaying schoolmarms, emblazoning *ain't* on their banners. In recording usage they were too often content with an undiscriminating nose count. They failed to consider a particular complication—popular attitudes toward common usage, such as strong feelings about *ain't,* which are an important part of the linguistic record. An English teacher ought to inform his students about such feelings even if he considers them unreasonable. And he may rightly feel a duty to discourage some usage growing acceptable. As another authority remarked, his subject properly includes "not only what *is* but what he thinks *ought to be.*"

But such concessions enabled Marckwardt to make a stronger case for the linguists. They can and now do take these complications into account, give subtler answers to problems of usage. They can better meet the charge that they are mere "relativists"—a sophisticated version of the objections raised because they complicated matters once considered simple and settled. Usage is in fact relative, appropriate language differing with situation and purpose as well as time and place, but this does not mean that we have no standards or no grounds for preferring one usage to another. The teacher then faces another complication in his personal preferences. He may not like, for instance, the substitution of *like* for *as,* though it has been common in speech for centuries and sanctioned by such distinguished writers as William Faulkner. He has then to face the problem of priorities, decide whether this violation of Standard English is as important as many others that students habitually indulge in. But at least linguistic studies can help him to make these decisions more sensitively and sensibly. And more humanely, in an awareness that children's addiction to linguistic error is not a form of original sin, and that millions of them in the schools now come from the other side of the railroad tracks. He must also "find a way of teaching the standard forms without stigmatizing those which represent the folk speech of the community."

On this latter point the seminar heartily concurred, because of its concern about handicapped children. David Mackay of Britain dwelt on the grievous harm done to a great many of these children by well-meaning teachers bent on saving them from linguistic sin. They are judged by their mistakes, too seldom by their achievements. The power slum children may have over language—often more striking than the verbal power of middle-class suburban children—is too often disregarded when not disapproved, so that their main tool of learning is blunted. Above all, they are made to feel different, inferior. Mackay cited another linguist on this injustice: "A speaker who is ashamed of his own language habits suffers a basic injury as a human being: to make anyone, especially a child, feel so ashamed is as indefensible as to make him ashamed of the color of his skin." And too often such linguistic intolerance comes down to social prejudice or snobbishness. In Britain the dedication of teachers to mistaken notions about Standard English reflects much older and deeper class feelings.

As an American teacher, Miriam Wilt drew much the same moral:

> The child has vocabulary; he has experiences; he has grammar; and he has *his* culture. Surely these are worth valuing and preserving. Surely these are worth using as a lever to broader, deeper, and richer goals. But more important, perhaps, than the school using what the child brings may be the effect upon the child's self-image of the school's use of what he brings. Dignity and self-respect accompany acceptance of him as he is. Proud of his heritage, he can begin to raise his sights so that his goal will always be just beyond his grasp. On the other hand, if everything he knows is wrong and everything he does is bad, he is apt to close his shell like an oyster and silently drift away to stand against the world of the school rather than with and of it.

The seminar accordingly debated the problem of just how to teach these children English. Some argued that we ought to drop the whole effort to teach them Standard English, which for them is a foreign dialect they can never feel at home with. The British (always the most vocal) were again inclined to oppose "intervening" in the child's development, but an American linguist joined them in protesting against tampering with a child's language, taking such risks of humiliating him. Standard English amounts to a bourgeois standard, and there is no reason why it must be taught to all students; English teachers should not cater to this bourgeois prejudice, give in to society's vulgar demands. Others cited the verdict of authorities that it is impossible anyway ever to take away a dialect with which children have grown up. Still others questioned the teaching of Standard English to such children simply as a matter of priorities: it takes an immense amount of time and energy, at the expense of other educational activities that might contribute more to their development. David Mackay had illustrated the common futility of the effort by a story about a teacher who was trying to teach his class to use *put* instead of *putten,* and was rewarded by an earnest youngster calling attention to his neighbor: "Look, sir, he's putten 'putten' and he should have putten 'put.' "

Yet those who defended the effort seemed to me no less humane, and rather more sensible. Standard English is not just a bourgeois dialect, after all, but the most common, widespread form of English, and no education for life in a democracy can be adequate without some knowledge of it. Call the preference for it ignorant or snobbish, the fact remains that it is the language of educated people everywhere, and no person can hope to talk or write appropriately and effectively for all his purposes unless he can use it with a fair degree of naturalness and correctness. Democratic idealism itself calls for the teaching of it to all children as an essential means to sharing in the heritage of their society and the opportunities for realizing their potentialities, bettering themselves both intellectually and socially. Refusing to teach it to poor children would automatically condemn most of them to remaining poor and underprivileged, seal the division into sheep and goats. If they will never entirely lose their native dialect, many of them manifestly can and do learn to speak Standard English well enough for social or working purposes. Our society is full of bilingual types, like telephone operators. At that most of them are not strictly bilingual, since there are many shades of dialect and degrees of mastery of Standard English. In the heterogeneous schools the seminar agreed were desirable, I would add, it would be impossible not to teach Standard English, or at least to protect poor children against the knowledge that their dialect was generally considered incorrect and inferior.

These differences of opinion could hardly be reconciled. But once more the differences illuminated the problem and brought out a significant measure of consensus, first on the need of more linguistic tolerance. All could agree that teachers should not at once begin nagging the young child about his mistakes, and that efforts to teach Standard English should be gradual, tactful, and respectful of the child, guided by the understanding of this dialect that linguists have given us; the real problem is to do the job well. All could appreciate the terrific problems of the schools in the slums and minority ghettos, where the most sympathetic teachers may be baffled by the apathy of many children, the sullenness or aggressiveness of many others. It was pointed out that desegregation is no automatic solution; selected Negro youngsters who were transferred to good white schools were still handicapped, unable to work to the best of their native abilities. Hence all applauded the recent efforts to face up to these problems. Only a few years ago, for example, all American primers were lily-white in text and illustration, and little Sambo served only for entertainment; now white and colored children mingle freely in text and drawings.

To me the spirit of this whole discussion was best exemplified in a report by Nelson Francis on a program he is in charge of to extend the abilities of Negro youths in Mississippi. Great pains are taken not to tamper with their dialect or to force another on them, but instead to provide them with alternatives in standards, spoken or written, and to discover their preferences; and so far they seem to enjoy the program. Although this report evidently did not convince those opposed to any tampering at all, and Francis as a linguist felt troubled by the liberties he was taking, I was struck by the extraordinary gentleness and tact of the program. That he was working with youths of eighteen and nineteen recalled a source of needless disagreement: the British were again thinking of the tender young "child," forgetting that youngsters in secondary school may be able to accept some correction of their language without being scarred for life.

Although the linguistic problem is basically much the same in both countries, class feeling is stronger and likely to be nastier in Britain. Nancy Mitford has remarked that "it is solely by its language that the upper class is clearly marked off from the others." At the seminar David Abercrombie dwelt on one expression of this feeling in a paper on English accents. "Accent" itself carries some stigma, since most people prefer to speak without one; but in fact all speakers of Standard English speak with an accent, depending on the country or commonly the region where they were born, and with foreigners on whether they have been taught American or British English. None can be called the "right" accent. England has a rare kind that linguists call "received pronunciation," unique in that it is not identified with any region. This is taught or acquired as the "best" accent, meaning "accepted in the best society." It is not clearly more agreeable to listen to than others, though it has long sounded so to British ears that American English grates on. Primarily it is cherished as "an accent of privilege and prestige" or, in short, a status symbol. It is another means of dividing the people—and stigmatizing the unprivileged.

In America the nearest equivalent, I suppose, is the New England accent, which in dictionaries was once recorded as the standard pronunciation (as of *half*), aped by some social or cultural climbers, and mistaken by many teachers as the "correct" accent. It was also ridiculed by ordinary Americans from other regions, however, and never became the standard accent of the educated. Abercrombie remarked that linguists are struck by the remarkable degree of uniformity in American speech. There is far less variety in regional dialects than in England, where the range of differences is wide enough to make people almost unintelligible to outsiders.[2] But as an English-speaking country America is strikingly different for another reason that is not generally realized. Joshua Fishman, a specialist in the sociology of language, called attention to this in a paper that illuminated the ambiguous attitudes of Americans toward language.

To begin with, English is not the mother tongue of about a tenth of white Americans; Mexican-American children are a considerable educational problem in the Southwest, as are Puerto Ricans in New York. An additional fifty to sixty million Americans belong to the first generation having English as their mother tongue and grew up in homes and neighborhoods where they heard some other language. Add the many millions more who belong to the second generation and heard the different language of their grandparents, and almost two thirds of the white population of America has been accounted for. "You do not have to scratch most white Americans very hard to elicit other than English sounds, other stress patterns, other rhythms, other verbal imagery and intonation—all with emotional connotations, complexly and simultaneously positive, negative, and ambivalent." In recent years many of these hybrid Americans have been reviving the language of their fathers, publishing more newspapers of their own, and demanding more bilingual schools. It is a nice question whether English teachers should try to capitalize on this linguistic wealth or ignore it, possi-

---

2 Here is a specimen of Norfolk English: "She's a fate mawther, but ollas in dibles wi the knacker and thackster." Translated into Standard English, "She's a clever girl, but always in trouble with the collar-maker and thatcher." To me the Norfolk version makes a more agreeable noise, but I assume that even those who oppose intervening or forcing Standard English on poor children might make an exception with such dialects.

bly even try to dispel the confusion; but in any case the problem remains how to go about dealing with it. Meanwhile a further complication for the profession is raised even by Americans whose roots in English are as much as three generations deep, for the largest segments of these are Negroes and rural southern whites—who alike present problems to the English teacher.

In short, Fishman concludes, "the English language in the United States is like the Mississippi River, a mile wide but frequently only an inch deep." Relatively few Americans love English or cherish it from the depths of their being as other peoples do their mother tongues; few handle it with the confidence and tenderness born of long, comfortable, deep association. Hence the peculiar difficulties of the English teacher. Many Americans tend to scorn cultivated speech and writing as fancy, effeminate, or highbrow. (So Adlai Stevenson, who in England would have been admired for his wit and style, was branded an "egghead," while Eisenhower's manhandling of the language only proved that he was "sincere.") At the same time, many have an uneasy concern about correctness as the clearest demonstration of mastery of the language, or at least worry about their spelling. The teacher too is likely to feel insecure and therefore excessively concerned with propriety.

It is the latter attitude that has governed the teaching of grammar—another fundamental matter about which linguists have much to say. In both Britain and America grammar has long been regarded by teachers and parents as absolutely essential, though by students as a dreadful bore. Practical Americans can least appreciate the ironical consequence, that what they have learned so laboriously is a kind of "poor man's Latin." When in the Renaissance Latin and Greek came to be the heart of higher education, what was taught was primarily the grammar of a dead language and then its literature. When centuries later the teaching of English came to be considered no less important, it took over its curriculum from the classics. English grammar was modeled on Latin grammar, from which it derived its rules. Latin was an unfortunate model, since English differs from it in fundamental respects, but the chief misfortune was the kind of grammar that was made standard in the eighteenth century. This was a rigid, authoritarian grammar in which the rules were regarded as absolute and fixed for all time, like the laws of nature or the commandments of God. It made no difference that people persisted in violating the rules, just as they disobeyed the commandments of God. This only proved that they were creatures of original sin.

We can now see that the chief victims of English teachers were the children of the poor, since they naturally used bad grammar. But all youngsters suffered from an endless barrage of do's and don't's, many of them arbitrary. Readers may recall the rules they once had to learn about the use of "shall" and "will," the reason why they should never say, "It's me," and the injunction never, never to split an infinitive—rules that the best writers had been disregarding for centuries. Apart from such arbitrariness, the teaching of grammar might still be justified as an intellectual discipline, especially needed in rude, slovenly America; and let us repeat that there is always need for standards of correctness. But the drilling was justified by another misconception. Far too many English teachers still assume that learning the parts of speech, memorizing the rules, parsing or diagraming sentences, and doing all the exercises that engrain such learning automatically improve the students' speaking and writing; or they may even believe that good grammar makes good writing. Recent studies have confirmed what should have been plain enough from the results over the generations, that the connection is negligible. Apart from its possible value as a mental discipline or as knowledge interesting for its own sake, the teaching of grammar has been chiefly a waste of time.

Since most teachers are still committed to the exercises,

and readers may not like to believe that what they went through in school as a matter of course was wasted effort, it may be well to repeat the elementary distinctions made by Nelson Francis in a report on the subject. Good grammar is not a matter of logic. One may ask, "Do you like this?" or reverse the question by, "Don't you like this?" and get the same answer—"No." Many a quite proper expression makes poor logic, as does this one—"many a." A writer has only to learn normal usage, not to think hard about it. Above all, grammar has nothing to do with style beyond the elementary proprieties. "I had hoped not to have to be beginning to explain" is strictly grammatical—and just as clumsy, for reasons a student would never gather from his grammar drill. Little if anything in the study of grammar will help him to speak or write more effectively.

Francis himself is nevertheless devoted to this study and excited by its present state. The prescriptive grammar that laid down the law for generations of students has for linguists long since been superseded, first by historical grammars that gave some idea how languages developed, then by grammars that attempted only to describe the present state of English, stirring up all the controversy over usage. Today the chief excitement appears to be over a new "generative" or "transformational" grammar, which is still in the making. I cannot pretend to be versed in this grammar, which was not expounded or discussed at the seminar. Looking over a book on it, I found it rather forbidding, with diagrams and formulas that at first glance looked like esoteric versions of the diagraming I once had to do. I have not been dazzled either, however, by a fleeting acquaintance with the new mathematics, which appears to be surviving some extravagance and disillusionment, and it seems that many English teachers are enthusiastic over the possibilities of the new grammar. But here the immediate question is: Will it help students any more to improve their writing than the old grammar did?

Some of the enthusiasts believe it will. Nelson Francis, however, believes that a theoretical knowledge of grammar "has no bearing at all upon the practice of writers." He remarked that he had never drawn on his own knowledge in writing his paper: "The hesitations and blank moments facing a motionless typewriter have all been due either to selection among words or selection among the alternative ways, all of them quite grammatical, in which a given idea may be expressed." Still, all experienced writers do know something about grammar, even though they have blessedly forgotten much of what they were taught, and one may wonder: Can students beyond the early grades be taught anything about writing unless they have some grammatical vocabulary, some conscious knowledge of the nature and structure of their language? The seminar agreed that teachers ought surely to have a sound knowledge of the language. What split it again was the question stated by Frank Whitehead: "Should any of this knowledge be taught, explicitly, to children, and if so at what stage?"

Most of the British characteristically wanted to minimize any such systematic teaching of language, at least before the age of fifteen or sixteen. Reacting violently against the arid routines, they held that an occasional, "implicit" teaching is enough; the teacher should introduce such knowledge only when the need arises from the work of the class. Again they brought up the young child's unconscious mastery of the structure of language as a model of "internalized" knowledge; normally the adult too uses language most effectively when unconscious of its structure. They pointed out that there was no evidence to support the assumption that systematic teaching of language improved writing. However desirable such knowledge may be, they added, the English teacher cannot do everything; he has to decide what is most important to teach in the limited time he has; and they concluded that explicit teaching about language should have a low priority.

Most of the linguists naturally inclined to think other-wise. They granted that they had no conclusive evidence yet of the utility of linguistic study, but they were content to defend it as a humanistic study. They stated as a fact that children have a natural curiosity about language, simply like to learn more about it. They maintained that the study of it could give older students a better understanding of mind, society, and culture—of themselves and their world. A com-mittee made up of two British linguists and two American nonlinguists presented this statement: "Linguistic knowl-edge—awareness of what words are, awareness of the way in which men seek to lay orderly verbal systems over against the confusion within themselves and beyond themselves, awareness of the extraordinary degree to which the cohesion of public life and private thought is a creation of the word—may not help the student to write splendid composi-tions, but can help him perceive himself more clearly as a composer of his experience, a maker of order." A linguist added that a conscious knowledge of language is especially important in an increasingly complex society that demands a more literate, articulate public than ever before. Another asked a pertinent question: *Can* one teach language "im-plicitly"? The real issue was when, what, and how much to teach.

It seemed to me that the British who held out for low priorities overlooked how much a teacher is bound to teach about language, and how much value they themselves saw in the contributions of linguists to a better understanding of it (not to mention the fact that most of their students leave school at the age of fifteen, when they thought it might be safe to teach language explicitly). Sitting in on a study group that had spent two fruitless sessions trying to agree on a statement of what a student should know by the time he completes secondary school, I made my one positive contri-bution to the seminar by drawing up a brief statement of the underlying agreement I thought they had reached:

The student should acquire some understanding of the nature of denotations and connotations of words. In view of the popular acceptance of the importance of learning to speak and write "good English," he should be made aware of the fluidity of language, variations in English, the existence of dialects, differences in standards, and the basis for standards. The fundamental importance of language in man's realizing his humanity and carrying on all his distinctive activities makes it desirable that the student have some awareness of this importance, and so far as possible some knowledge of the nature, structure, and history of English. The study of language—as of literature—need not be confined to its practical uses, but may be justified simply as a humanistic study, valuable in itself. Those who agree but object that priorities in the classroom make it impossible to devote time to this study may nevertheless admit that teachers inevitably talk a good deal about language anyway, and that by common consent many of them have been wasting much time in unprofitable exercises and the teaching of obsolete grammar resting upon outmoded assumptions about language.

Although neither side was completely satisfied with this statement, both were willing to sign it. News of the agreement brought some congratulations from other participants.

This triumph was short-lived, however. In the final discussions of the seminar disaster struck: the circulation of a digest of a proposed program in English grammar put out by an American state university. It looked just as dreary as the old exercises in grammar. The British were appalled by it; they wanted to know how these ghastly exercises could be considered "humanistic." The linguists themselves were embarrassed by it, quickly disowning it. Only two Americans put in a defensive word for it. I mention it chiefly to illustrate the limitations and the dangers of linguistics. Since this is a youthful science, its practitioners are likely to claim too much for it, or at least for its value in the teaching of English. Especially in America their fondness for systematic study may support an already excessive faith in program or system. This particular program looked no better for the assurance that it was "experimental" and that a lot of research was going on to check up on the results, presumably make it more "scientific." Meanwhile the clearest contribution of linguistics to the teaching of English remains its studies of usage, not the new modes in grammatical exercises.

Yet this little tempest clouded the main issue. It struck linguistics at its weakest point, not its basic claims to importance. The linguists themselves led away from these claims when they rightly pointed out that while they had no weighty research evidence to support them, neither did their critics to support their own claims that "implicit" teaching is enough, or for that matter their preferences in the teaching of literature. I doubt that research can prove the value of linguistics as a humanistic study, good for its own sake, any more than it can prove the value of literature. Nevertheless I have no doubt of this value. Language has as sound claims to proper understanding as do mathematics and science, for certainly it is as fundamental. And I would make more than the linguists did of the fascination of their subject, or the fun and the hell of it—the pleasure a child gets in satisfying his natural curiosity about language, and as he grows up in getting a live sense of its possible delights, its wonders and mysteries, even its terrors. Barbara Strang observed that if elements in the repertoire of interest, curiosity, and delight that a child brings to school are not developed and used in his education, they tend to die—"and, like other dead material, not to vanish, but to degenerate into something nasty." A neglect of his natural interests in language will not kill all his pleasure in its uses but may expose him to the tawdry, corrupt uses featured by the mass media at their worst.

At the end I should emphasize the significant agreement underlying the quarrels at the seminar. These were family quarrels, of people not really separated or seeking divorce.

73

Because no one questioned the importance of the contributions of the linguists, it was easy to overlook how revolutionary they are. They have profoundly altered not only the content of language study but attitudes toward language. They have demonstrated unmistakably that popular ideas about "good English" are trivial and shallow when not false. There remains the unanswerable question of just when, what, and how much to teach about the language, but the agreement of the seminar that English teachers need to have a sound, conscious knowledge of the language means that most teachers need to be retrained and the English curriculum drastically revised.

CHAPTER FIVE

THE USES
OF LITERATURE

"The case for literature," wrote Denys Thompson, "is that it stands for humanity at a time when the human values are not upheld, as they used to be, by religion and the home, or even by education itself as a whole." Although a number of papers at the seminar touched on the value of literature, especially for modern society, this issue was not debated. Everyone (including the harried linguists) appeared to take for granted the case for it, to feel no need of either attacking or justifying its traditionally high place in the English curriculum, which in the high schools gives much more time to it than to composition or language study. Discussion centered rather on the questions of what literature should be taught, for what purposes, and how. The consensus stood basically for literature for its own sake, as its own reward.

I think more attention might have been given to its broad social values, inasmuch as most Americans preoccupied with the national interest in education regard literature as not really a vital need, or as useful chiefly because it may improve "communication skills."[1] The discussions could sound rather academic at times, more concerned about the purity or autonomy of literature than the interests of students. As I review them, I shall indicate some possible oversights and confusions. But I also think that for the most part the seminar was saying what most needs to be said, to both English teachers and the general public. The teaching of English in the schools too often confirms the public interest primarily in the conventional uses of literature, as a means of inculcating the sanctity of the flag, home, religion, and private property—the heart of the American Way of Life. In particular it is saddled with routine practices that do not further the best interests of either literature or students. Readers who once had to plow through *Silas Marner* might find the discussions refreshing. At least the consensus settled on some surprising recommendations, which would again mean a curriculum quite different from the current one in most schools.

Most of the study groups gave some attention to literature since it has long been at or near the heart of the English curriculum, and nobody wanted to separate it sharply from other interests or skills; some held that it was the best means to improving writing. The group that focused on it was at first somewhat uneasy over the assigned topic, "Response to Literature," which might suggest a passive, merely verbal, or immediate response; but they decided that their concern was an active response, with deep, lasting effects. Specifically, their main concern became the contribution of literature to

---

[1] When Congress in 1964 was debating federal support of institutes for English teachers, one congressman tried to exclude the teaching of literature by substituting "language arts" for English. At that he was old-fashioned, using "arts" instead of "skills."

the development of the child, on essentially the premise stated by Frank Whitehead in *The Disappearing Dais*: "All children, whatever their ultimate role in life is to be, need experience of literature . . . if their personalities are to expand and flower into a capacity for fulness of living." The immediate object of the teacher should be to get the child actively "involved" or "engaged"—a favorite theme at the seminar. In simpler terms, the teacher should make or keep literature alive, as it naturally is for little children. He should as naturally assist the growing child to read with more understanding, or to achieve the "proficiency" that appeared as a primary aim in the statements of several groups, but most at the seminar actually wanted more than this. If they seldom put it first in so many words, their principal aim was that students acquire not merely an ability to read well but a lasting desire to read books—a love of literature that in America may brand a teenager as "queer."

On the question what literature should be taught, the seminar took a broad view, with surprisingly little debate considering the popular tendency in America to make the English curriculum a dumping ground. Several groups reported independently that the curriculum should include not only English and American literature but the "reservoir" literature in the background of our culture (such as classical mythology, European folk and fairy tales, and the Bible), some foreign literature in translation, and some attention to other media of expression, such as moving pictures, radio, and television—altogether a quite ambitious program. As for literature proper, it was assumed that "good" books should be assigned, but the seminar took a broad view of these too, not insisting on the classics or anything like a "great books" program. Some standard works (such as *Silas Marner*) have long been assigned out of unthinking habit, without regard to the interests of students. The literature study group specifically questioned the assumption that our cultural heritage required the teaching of certain writers.

79

While some writers, from Chaucer and Shakespeare to Mark Twain, D. H. Lawrence, and Robert Frost, have "provided rich literary experiences to readers of varied backgrounds," this heritage "is not a packet to be transmitted inert," but is alive and fluid. "Each generation takes from it what it needs and adds to it in its turn." The chairman of the group observed that they were like an airplane, serene when cruising at high altitudes, uneasy when coming down to earth; but despite some uneasiness they refused to commit themselves to the proposition that any one writer—even Shakespeare— must be included in the curriculum. An American might have remarked that a play or two of Shakespeare are about the only classics that many high school students read.

As unconventional a conclusion emerged from a familiar theme of discussion. The British as usual frowned on the traditional teaching of knowledge about literature, in particular literary history, but on this matter they had most of the Americans with them. Americans agreed that the schools have been teaching far too much inert knowledge, such as names and dates. One pointed out that literary history has no sound claim to be required of all students when physics is not. James Squire collaborated on a statement that went further, rejecting such courses as the history of American literature, English literature, and world literature—courses like those given in college, which have been growing more common now that the high schools are preparing more students for college. The applause over this demolition of the standard curriculum drowned out the doubts ventured by one or two who wondered (as I did) whether our schools really should stop teaching American literature. The statement was greeted most enthusiastically by Benjamin De-Mott, who throughout the seminar played with great gusto the role of *enfant terrible,* insisting that the Establishment was killing English. He thought it all right for teachers to start with any work, even *Playboy,* so long as they made a point of relating it vitally to the student's experience.

80

"Experience"—always an honorific word in America, whose writers have often sacrificed literary form and style to life—was upheld by the British too as a criterion in selecting appropriate literature to assign. Denys Thompson cited with approval a Yorkshire teacher: "We must continually aim at giving the children experiences through which they will develop. . . . We must think less in terms of the subjects a child must learn and more in terms of experiences they can enjoy and gain interest from." A joint Anglo-American paper suggested that the English curriculum might be designed in terms of experience rather than knowledge, with such criteria as variety, points of view or perspectives on life, and kinds of experience ("crude examples: being a savior, being alone, being rejected; home, growing up, leaving home"). If the knowledge resulting from such a curriculum might have gaps in it, the child's expanding perception of the world would enable him to fill the gaps for himself; whereas if we make knowledge primary we can avoid the gaps, but may fail to develop the child's capacity to use language as a means of extending his knowledge himself. Benjamin DeMott hailed this statement as dynamite—it blew "literature" right out the window. The members of the literature study group were more circumspect, or more devoted to the traditional values of literature, as they took up the problem of a continuous, cumulative curriculum in literature; but they too were concerned primarily with the expansion of the child's experience, not of his formal knowledge of literature.

In an introductory paper on "Response to Literature," James Britton wrote that the teacher's aim should be to refine and develop responses children are already making, as to fairy tales and nursery rhymes, and to open doors, introduce them to a greater range and diversity of literary works, provide the enlargement of experience they themselves naturally want. The study group thought that up to the age of about eleven the problems of teaching literature are not

81

formidable, because children respond directly and unashamedly to both poetry and fiction. By then, however, they have become more extroverted and thereafter are more guarded in their responses; they may not want to get "involved" in love poems, for instance. With adolescents the problems grow much harder. They shy away from expressing their emotions just because they are emotionally disturbed, or even though they may have very sentimental responses. They may welcome the opportunity of discussing the emotional problems of their age group, but resent any expectation that they do so. They are also beginning to anticipate adulthood and are inclined to adopt some adult attitudes. Hence they may ask the "practical" question: What's the good of all this literature? They may seek the safety of conformity, and they tend to read less widely by themselves, giving more time and thought to social life. The study group offered no solution to these problems, except to say that reading materials should always be chosen for their literary value rather than their possible bearing on psychological problems.

This possibly inconsistent subordination of the adolescent's development or inner experience to the claims of literature suggested a complication that from the outset faces curriculum makers. The study group was never so bold as to lay out a specific curriculum, commit itself to any "right book for the right time," inasmuch as children have different needs and develop at different rates, in different ways. The group might have made more of the impossibility of agreement among teachers, which was dramatized when the seminar took time off to analyze and discuss a poem by Thomas Hardy, "The Man He Killed":[2]

---

[2] Reprinted from *Collected Poems of Thomas Hardy* by permission of The Hardy Estate, Macmillan & Co., Ltd., London and The Macmillan Company of Canada Limited.

"Had he and I but met
     By some old ancient inn,
We should have sat us down to wet
     Right many a nipperkin!

"But ranged as infantry,
     And staring face to face,
I shot at him as he at me,
     And killed him in his place.

"I shot him dead because—
     Because he was my foe,
Just so: my foe of course he was;
     That's clear enough; although

"He thought he'd 'list, perhaps,
     Offhand like—just as I—
Was out of work—had sold his traps—
     No other reason why.

"Yes; quaint and curious war is!
     You shoot a fellow down
You'd treat if met where any bar is,
     Or help to half-a-crown."

While no one considered this a great poem, some thought it
was a pretty good one, especially the third stanza, or at least
good enough for thirteen-year-olds working their way toward the best in poetry; others thought it was pretty bad,
phony in its archaic poetic diction ("old ancient," "foe,"
"quaint and curious"). Some thought it was too bad to teach
at all; and the rest disagreed on how it should be taught,
whether with emphasis on the poet's intention, the perti-
nence of the theme today, the teacher's idea of its literary
merits or faults, or what have you.[3]

---

[3] What I had was some embarrassment, for I used to read the poem
with pleasure to college freshmen. I was not troubled, however, by an

But all along the study group—like the seminar as a whole—might have been embarrassed more than they appeared to be by their dual objective. They agreed that the teacher should choose reading that is meaningful, interesting, and enjoyable to children, but also that he should try tactfully to improve their tastes, make them more concerned about quality, and lead them toward "the full range of literary experience that he himself can compass." By the age of sixteen or seventeen their education "should provide some introduction to imaginative literature of the highest order." An American might note again that too many high school students graduate (as my sons did) with virtually no such introduction; they read anthologies containing chiefly short works, many of them ephemeral, with perhaps some longer ones much abridged or emasculated. The worry expressed over courses in American, English, and world literature could seem excessive. Given the wide range and rich variety of our literary tradition, I would stress both the possibility and the need of selecting some great works of the past that students can find meaningful and enjoyable.

Another problem brought out more difference between the two countries. The British aversion to teaching knowledge about literature extended to knowledge of literary forms, genres, and techniques. Frank Whitehead dismissed, for example, Northrop Frye's proposal that the curriculum be organized by the "pre-generic forms" he makes out—Comedy, Romance, Tragedy, Irony—emphasizing the first two forms in the early years, the last two in the later years. The study group made nothing of this or any other structural principle to plan a cumulative curriculum. Since the

---

objection an American raised to assigning the poem, that it had too many British locutions that an American student would not understand. From my experience students do not expect to understand all the words in poetry, even poetry they like—just as people who read the Bible can read what Jesus said about "sinners and publicans" without ever wondering what a "publican" was.

British wished to introduce students to the whole range of literary experience, they naturally included some teaching about literary forms and genres, but again they wished to keep this casual and unobtrusive, not systematic or "explicit." Similarly they inclined to agree with Whitehead in playing down knowledge of techniques, how writers gain their effects. He insisted that such knowledge is not the same thing as "being able to experience these effects as fully as possible," and that too many teachers consider it worth having for its own sake. Americans were on the whole more inclined to agree with Robert Heilman's statement quoted by Albert Kitzhaber: "The idea that knowledge follows interest is a scandalous half-truth," and "it is a better-than-half-truth that *interest follows knowledge*." As it is, most American students have too little general knowledge of and about literature.

Whitehead took what seemed to me a more dubious stand when he dismissed efforts to order the literary curriculum by basic themes, such as the relationships of man to deity, to other men, to nature, and to himself. He objected that this approach "leads our attention away from the unique work of literature"—for him always the first and last concern—towards features that may be abstracted from it, link it with other works, and so lead to his *bête noire*, knowledge *about* literature. I assume that children have no natural reverence for the unique work of art, and except for the few who are destined to be majors in English, I see no absolute need of their acquiring it at any cost.[4] Students are normally interested in basic themes, familiar ideas in a literary work, its connections with other works and broadly with life. Especially at a time when the study of literature is considered impractical and superfluous, it would seem poor

---

[4] Readers should be warned that I am myself a kind of renegade from literary criticism, having written chiefly about history in the last twenty years. This is another of my doubtful qualifications for writing this report.

strategy to play up its unique aesthetic qualities at the expense of its relevance to basic problems and common interests. And something is to be said even for the crude tactics most English teachers use. One participant complained of such common questions as, "Why do we admire Brutus in spite of his failure more than the successful Mark Antony?" This is of course no way to make students appreciate the greatness or uniqueness of Shakespeare; but as Benjamin DeMott protested, it is one way of making his plays more meaningful to young students, relating them to vital interests. It should be no sin to talk about what literature is about.

The British quite agreed, however, that the aim of an English teacher is not to turn out little literary critics; and here indeed they swung further to the left than most Americans. While they of course want students to become more discriminating and consciously critical, they stressed the dangers of making them formulate their response too early. As George Allen wrote, "The pupils are expected to learn the right things to say or to write about what they read, rather than to enjoy the experience itself." The right things are what the textbook says or the teacher expects; so they distrust their own responses, the independent judgment that should count most. James Britton wrote that probably more harm has been done to the cause of literature in this way than any other. "To have children, for whatever reason, take over from their teachers the analysis of a work of literature which their teachers in turn have taken over from the critics or from their English professors—this is not a short cut to literary sophistication; it is a short circuit that fuses the whole system." Or as Benjamin DeMott put it in a final statement of his credo: "Everyone takes in, by implication, that this is the subject: the first fact about literature is that there is good stuff and bad stuff and teacher knows the good stuff. (The bad stuff is what other people read.) And teacher will tell you which is which even if you don't ask."

The problem, then, is to decide at what stage the formulation of critical judgment should start. The British, thinking of the youngster as a "child" until he is fifteen or sixteen, seemed to think that it should be postponed until that age. If so, they were again ducking the problem with most of their children, who leave school at that age. Most of the Americans seemed inclined to start earlier and do more. Since there is always much talk about literature going on in the classroom, some explicit teaching about literary forms and critical vocabulary would make it more pointed, disciplined talk. One might apply to all high school students what James Britton granted of "most adults," that a reader's responses are sharpened if they are "in some measure" formulated. But here, as always, one must depend on the teacher's tact.

The American attitude reflected a modified influence of the so-called New Critics, who for some years were the reigning fashion in literary criticism. English departments in the universities had been turning out mostly literary scholars, distinguished by their historical knowledge about literature rather than sensitive appreciation of it, and they thereby had an unfortunate influence on the teaching of literature in the schools. The New Critics helped to turn young men to the study of literature as literature, or works of art. They called for a close formal analysis of what they called the poem "in itself"—detached from history, society, or the biography of the poet. Both the British and the Americans at the seminar welcomed their stress on aesthetic values and closer reading. They also mostly agreed, however, that the New Critics were too schematic and called for too much explicit analysis, which again amounted to learning about literature and might interfere with the enjoyment of it, the direct personal response of the student. (In De-Mott's words, these critics made a poem "a fascinating clockworks that told no time.") The seminar did not brood as much as might have been expected over the conspicuous problem today, that students read much less outside the classroom than they used to, and practically no poetry at all; but the feeling was that teachers should try to stimulate wide as well as close reading. As James Britton wrote, the objective was both to get students to "read *more books* with satisfaction" and to "read books with *more satisfaction*." In this spirit many shared something of DeMott's animus against both "lit. hist." and "lit. crit."

The apparent consensus was summed up in a joint statement on "Response and Formulation" by Wallace Douglas of America and Barbara Hardy of England, which was highly praised. I cite a representative passage by Mrs. Hardy:

> Affective responses come from people who are not necessarily organized and complete, and literary response, at school and college, is often crazily expected to come off in the same way in different people responding to literature from widely different periods and cultures. Response is a word that reminds the teacher that the experience of art is a thing of our making, an activity in which we are our own interpretative artist. The dryness of schematic analysis of imagery, symbols, myth, structural relations, *et al.* should be avoided passionately at school and often at college. *It is literature, not literary criticism, which is the subject.* It is vividly plain that it is much easier to teach literary criticism than to teach literature, just as it is easier to teach children to write according to abstract models of correctness than to use their own voices.

All this discussion, however, centered on the appreciation and enjoyment of particular works, without relation to the cultural heritage. The study group offered another joint Anglo-American statement on the teacher's responsibility to this heritage, but it was very brief and inconclusive. It ended:

> It may be that no single literary work is so important that it must be read by all students; there are bound to be

gaps in individual experiences. But any literary education should include, say, some acquaintance with Chaucer, Shakespeare, some of the romantic poets, and the major fiction of the past two centuries. Without contact with his literary heritage, can an American really be an American, or an Englishman an Englishman?

The group offered no answer to this question, and in its summary report dropped the suggestion that a literary education had to include certain writers. On this matter I think the group—and the seminar as a whole—slighted the needs of not only "society" but also students.

Frank Whitehead observed that with older students literature should be read "in context," this being knowledge about the author and his other works, the conditions of his time, and his relationship to other writers; but he added his belief that such knowledge contributed relatively little to our understanding and enjoyment of a work of literature, and could not justify historical survey courses. It was again only the particular literary work that mattered, not its importance in our literary heritage. Most others who wrote or spoke about the teaching of literature apparently thought likewise. Their emphasis was on what growing children were interested in and could enjoy, not what they possibly needed to read as they grew up, especially when they were old enough for some of the greater writers of the past. Most of the British went no further than one who remarked that the classics should not be forced on students, but should at least be brought into the classroom and left lying around. Glyn Lewis could sound like a voice crying in the wilderness as he alone kept insisting on the claims of our heritage, repeating the elementary truths that the unique literary works are also products of a cultural tradition and the unique child grows up and learns within a particular culture.

Thus Lewis pointed out that the seminar was expressing much concern over disadvantaged children, the need of respecting their dialect and all they brought from the traditions of their subculture—a concern he fully shared; but he added that we needed as well to respect the great tradition and the great culture, which were superior to the little ones. So far as possible, teachers should make these available to the "disadvantaged" children, give them a greater, richer world to grow up in. But all children need some sense of community in a divided society, sense of unity in a heterogeneous society, just as the nation needs a basically united people. They need to realize that "each new generation is not a new people: we are what we are because we are able to share in a past, in a common heritage, not simply because of our ability to communicate in the present or share the excitement of innovation." As for literature, the "context" of the greater works is not merely incidental to understanding but important in its own right, and both it and the work itself may help to develop historical imagination, another means to maturity. And so forth, including the value of knowing something too about the history of the English language.

The seminar paid scant attention to a report in which Lewis developed such truisms to balance the personal, individual needs of growing children. Nevertheless the truisms define an important aim that has been neglected in the teaching of literature, above all in America. Although several Americans echoed from time to time the common complaints about the many high schools that offer only a smattering of literature, mostly modern, I would emphasize much more their deficiencies in the teaching of both literature and history. From my experience, most students entering college have little sense of American literary tradition, still less sense of the past in general. They accordingly have as little perspective on the contemporary scene that has provided most of the subject matter they studied. As for the spreading courses in American, English, and world literature, these are no doubt mostly superficial, but not necessarily so. As I see it, the main problem is to teach them primarily as literature, not history, yet with an eye to developing historical imagination, or simply historical sense. They should deal intensively with a number of representative works instead of attempting to "cover" the whole subject.

Another problem that Glyn Lewis tried to keep in balance was the need of taking into account both "the cognitive and affective development" of children. These technical terms, which cropped up in many a paper, tended to obscure some simplicities. The literature study group discussed chiefly "affective" responses, since they were wary of knowledge, explicit analysis, demands for "formulation" of response, etc. They nevertheless assumed, at least tacitly, that literature itself is a significant way of "knowing" about life. Lewis stressed more both the need of knowledge about literature and the responsibilities of the knowledge claimed for literature. He even spoke of the importance of leading children toward the "truth," not merely toward wider experience. This word was seldom used at the seminar, I suppose because of an awareness that it is used much too loosely and may sound rhetorical. At any rate, there was little talk about such matters as developing powers of logical analysis in reading, helping students to detect fallacy, semantic confusion, or mere blah-blah. It is hard to avoid using the slippery word "truth" even in talking about imaginative literature, for one common way of describing the cheap fiction that youngsters become addicted to is to say that the view of life presented—how boy wins girl, good guys always beat bad guys, and the rest—is shallow, distorted, false, or in a word *un*true.

A related problem was taken up in another summary report that the seminar did not discuss, one by James Miller on "Literature and Values." Frank Whitehead commented in a different connection that the experience of good reading can itself do the job of education in values, but I gathered that the main reason why Miller's paper was ignored was that no one seriously disagreed with it. Possibly, too, some were embarrassed by his explicit use of the old-fashioned word "moral." His thesis, at any rate, was that all literary works embody some vision of life, system of values, or moral dimension, and that although this dimension is not the key to their artistic value, it calls for moral imagination in good reading. It creates something of a problem with many of the world's classics (even the Old Testament), which embody beliefs remote from ours, likely to be uncongenial to students; to read them well calls for both historical sense and moral imagination. As it is, Miller observed, the teaching of literature is beset by two fatal tendencies. One is to treat the moral dimension as if it were the sole end of literature, to extract it, to divorce it from the work of art, and to offer it to students as abstract truth. The other is "to avoid the difficulties and dangers of discussing the moral dimension by ignoring it and concentrating on formal, aesthetic, structural, or other elements." Both impoverish literature and are likely to bore students.

The tendency to ignore moral issues is understandable as a revulsion against the popular demand for wholesome morals in literature. One study group was presented with a list of basic values, as a guide to teachers, that represented the consensus of many educators. It included the worth of the individual, the brotherhood of man, the consent of the governed, devotion to truth, moral equality, moral responsibility, the pursuit of life, liberty, and happiness, respect for excellence, and spiritual enrichment. A believer in democracy should esteem all these values; but someone expressed the consensus of the group when he said that the list scared the hell out of him. The thought of turning ordinary teachers loose on these objectives might scare anyone who cherishes literature.

The main problem today is obviously the tendency to make too much of the moral issues in literature, at the expense of its literary values. This is more dangerous because of the popular demand for simple, conventional morals, and the fear of books that are disturbing, "subversive," or "un-American." Salinger's *The Catcher in the Rye,* for example, upset many parents and was banned in many schools; but its popularity with teenagers seemed to me especially heartening, apart from the literary merits of the book, as a sign that they do not have such a passion for becoming well adjusted as appears when they answer questionnaires. James Miller concluded that teachers of literature should select books embodying diverse visions of life and beliefs about values, and then question, discuss, and explore them with the students; this would lead to an awareness of moral complexity, ambiguity, and paradox. The seminar expressed no objection to this conclusion. Still, it is not so harmless as may appear: the public does not cherish complexity or ambiguity either.

As a teacher I am disposed to introduce this whole issue of diverse, conflicting values quite explicitly, meeting it head-on. With students in the last two years of high school, whom I do not think of as "children," it seems to me desirable to link the issue with democratic theory about the individual and the pluralistic, open society, and with some effort to give a historical perspective, develop historical imagination. The "philosophy" that is being sought to guide teachers of literature might well include more specific consideration of the relations of the individual and a democratic society. I would have seniors read, for instance, De Tocqueville's classic *Democracy in America*—a kind of work that no study group considered in its report. But for this reason I repeat that in general the seminar dwelt on what most needs to be said today. It was seeking development of the individuality that is threatened by the pressures to conformity in mass education. It was concerned with aesthetic values that do not seem like a real human need in a commercialized industrial society where a vast deal of tawdriness, drabness, and ugliness is accepted as natural and normal. This is not the time or place for an essay on what modern technology is doing to people, as well as for them;

but the study of literature as recommended by the seminar might give a better idea why a people with by far the highest standard of living in all history is not clearly the happiest people on earth.

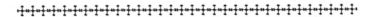

CHAPTER SIX

WRITING
AND TALKING

Composition, wrote Frank Whitehead, hangs round our neck like the albatross. It has long been a burden for both teachers and students, often the heaviest burden; but apparently there is no getting rid of it. Hence Miriam Wilt raised the question: *Why* all this composition over the many school years? "Of those sixty out of a hundred young people who finally show up in Freshman Composition class, how many will ever need or wish to write again except for those interminable term papers? . . . Why spend all of this precious school time perfecting a skill that will seldom or never be used?" In later life even those who come up in the world will spend most of their time talking and listening, seldom writing. And why, in particular, *themes?* Compositions of a few hundred words, a kind that students will never write again, and for the best of which there is no literary market?

Yet an immense amount of time and effort goes into teaching students composition. It may seem more wasteful because the farther they go, the plainer it becomes that many of them are nonwriters. They might seem to have been born nonwriters except for another token of futility. English teachers go on as if they agreed with the general public that composition is absolutely essential, much more important and practical than literature; yet on the record nothing in English is taught less effectively, amid more confusion and conflict of theory, or hunch.

The seminar did not debate Miss Wilt's pertinent questions. From all appearances it took for granted that composition is indispensable, the albatross immortal. Although no one study group dedicated itself to the subject, various groups discussed composition as a necessary part of English; none proposed doing away with it. The main concern was how to teach it more effectively. And though I think the questions might have been given more attention, I suppose there is no real question that something like composition is essential. It is a practical necessity because all students have to do considerable writing in other courses too, as on papers and tests, and still more in college. In later life almost all will at least write letters, and many will have to do some kind of writing for their business or professional purposes. More important, by this effort students at least learn more about language, something about how to express various kinds of ideas, and so about how to think.

Characteristically the seminar was most interested in the value of composition for the development of children. By writing they learn how to order and shape their experience, thereby learning more about life and themselves. As for the question how to teach composition more effectively, there were various suggestions, but the basic one was the same as for reading. It was to get students more "involved" or "engaged" in their writing.

For this reason some student themes presented by a

panel of visiting high school teachers made a generally poor impression. One was a close interpretation of a sonnet by Rossetti, which the teacher had graded A+. Most of the discussants thought it was sometimes sensitive but too often gushing or false (Benjamin DeMott said it was simply awful); they considered it a poor kind of assignment, almost bound to call out strained, artificial writing. A personal narrative that had pleased the teacher likewise struck some as too much like a writing exercise or dummy run. Almost all were appalled by some "average" samples of evaluation reports offered by a teacher who seemed pleased with the results of this kind of assignment. The average ran like this report of a car wash held by a Bible class:

> One reason for our success was the overwhelming enthusiasm for the project by all our members. At all our preliminary meetings there was at least a seventy-five percent turnout. Everyone contributed useful ideas and was anxious to help in any way possible. Participation in the actual car wash itself was gratifying. . . . The organization committee did a wonderful job in organizing the car wash. . . . Outstanding evidence of the good planning was the extensive advertising campaign which was carried out so successfully before the car wash.

All agreed in blaming this dreary prose on the assignment, which drove the student to clichés. DeMott said it was only a dreadful example of how most of what is taught in English is unreal or dead. I was depressed by the thought that such writing is all too real—the assignment could be called practical because this is the way club presidents and secretaries, young and old, gratify their members all over the land.

The seminar was as hard on the universities. One report traced the faults of high school teaching to Freshman English, which almost all teachers have memories of, and most are now preparing their students for. Although it takes various forms (and I think has been generally improved in recent years), it has typically centered on composition, especially in the state universities and technical schools, where it is known as a "service" course (though not in an animal husbandry sense). After a review of grammar, punctuation, and sentence structure, the student settles down to a series of "papers" with the help of a handbook. The papers are in various modes—exposition, description, argument, literary analysis, etc.—and often culminate in a research paper. After a year of such tests or trials, each corrected and graded, the student is supposed to be able to do college work, write competently in any course. One reason why he is nevertheless often a dull, awkward writer is that the trials are too artificial. Prescribed themes of three hundred words, which ease his burden and the teacher's by their brevity, do not permit him to develop his subject freely or fully. For each different assignment the instructor (usually a graduate assistant) gives some general suggestions, but is unlikely to take time—or have the time—to prepare for it by a lively class discussion that might make the assignment more meaningful. Most students regard the "paper" as a chore, which they perform more or less conscientiously in order to get a decent grade, but too seldom with their heart in it or their whole mind on it. In too many papers they go nowhere in particular because they started with nothing in particular to say and no real desire to say it. They know well enough that writing well is hard work, but not that the effort can be exciting.

Hence the problem is how to get them really involved (or as the educationists now say, "motivated"). There is no easy answer, of course, and no one way that is clearly the best way. The seminar considered some possible good ways, but agreed chiefly on what were wrong ones. In the schools both ways start with young children, whom it is relatively easy to get interested in writing or expressing themselves.

In the first place, children need an audience other than the teacher. They write most easily when they write for the class, are entertained and stimulated by one another's fancies. English teachers forget that with older children an audience is no less important. As Wendell Johnson has complained, teachers fail because they appear to emphasize "writing" instead of writing-about-something-for-someone: "You cannot write writing." Too often they assign the youngsters literary topics for which there can hardly be a live audience except the teacher himself. Meanwhile they have fallen into the routine ways that were deplored in other discussions. They weaken children's confidence by stressing their errors, stifle their interest by making correctness the main end. They set them to doing grammatical exercises from which they can get no intellectual satisfaction except the achievement of correctness. Pride in good grammar scarcely leads to pleasure in good writing.

Older children, however, bring up the usual difficulties that make impossible the hope of an ideal cumulative curriculum in English. Although much has been written about the "stages" of literacy, linguists at the seminar reported that it is mostly rubbish. English teachers have in any case to deal with a development that is not simple and uniform. In writing, Frank Whitehead observed, it is not a direct movement from simple to more complex, crude to more refined. Others ventured that there is no clear criterion for "effective" writing, which the seminar preferred to "correct" as the main aim. More complex sentences and a larger vocabulary are signs of development, but they do not guarantee effectiveness; else there would be much more satisfaction with the writing of older children. Similarly with their growing capacity for abstract thought, which teachers naturally seek to bring out in their writing. This capacity develops slowly in many children, it does not exhilarate them all as theme writers, it requires a great deal of other learning before they can write good essays of ideas, and it does not supplant their need or desire for personal, concrete writing. It does not simply exhilarate either teachers of composition, who are likely to be less interested in the abstract ideas of older children than in the personal writing of young ones; so it leads to more assignments that produce chiefly canned themes, written to satisfy the teacher but to please nobody else, including the writer.

As for methods of teaching composition, research has been of little help. A study made of some five hundred research projects (with the aid of a munificent grant of $13,345 by the U.S. Office of Education) revealed chiefly how inconclusive most of the findings were. The clearest agreement was again that the study of traditional grammar had a negligible effect on the improvement of writing, or even a harmful one, since it takes up time that might have been spent in practicing writing. Little study has been made of the effects of all the correcting and grading on which teachers spend so much of their time. My guess is that students might improve more if they were split up into groups and simply practiced writing for and on one another, now and then bringing to the teacher what they considered their best efforts; but I suppose no experiment could conclusively prove this.

It was on the problems of dealing with secondary or high school students that the seminar again tended to split into two camps. The British inclined to trust to the aid of literature to keep students interested in writing, and in composition to the stimulus of personal, creative writing—the subject of the next chapter. The Americans were more concerned about the practical necessity of training in exposition, the kind of writing students have to do in other courses, and later on in professional memoranda and reports. Exposition raises the problem of how to lead to it from the personal writing and imaginative literature students begin with, and how to get and keep them "involved" in writing factual reports or explanations. Several Americans proposed that the curriculum be centered on rhetoric, the basic principles of the effective use of language, which would be a means of uniting writing, speaking, and reading; but the British remained cool to this idea. They had a possible excuse in an unsigned paper that made the rounds, a detailed outline of "The Act of Composing." It began:

A. The writer and his idea
  1. Setting a frame
    a) Utilizing traditional patterns of prose
      1) Description

Two or three dozen numerals and little letters followed under A and then B, C, and D (the writer and his audience, his style, and his total purpose)—all very tidy, but unlikely to get either teachers or students excited about the act of composing, or to help much anyone engaged in it.

The seminar did not discuss a particular problem that Harold Rosen of England brought up—the demand for "impersonal" language. In all subjects other than English, he pointed out, students are bombarded with such language, and as they go up in school the bombardment mounts. It presumes "an unknown audience about whom the only valid assumption is that they want access to the ideas, data, etc., without ambiguity and subjectivity"; i.e., the writer is expected to keep out of his work. For young students this means in effect learning a new language, at first alien, and in writing it the question of what they are writing for. "What kind of urgent pressure to write exists in a setting where, in fact, they are usually writing for a teacher who knows it all anyway?" One might say that this problem should be left to the teachers of these other subjects. Our schools assume, however, that it is the job of the English teacher alone to teach students how to write, and if he gives them no training in impersonal writing, the chances are that nobody will. The popular idea is that except perhaps for some technical terms this is "simple prose." Students know better, since they read almost nothing but impersonal language in all their textbooks—whose authors, Rosen added, often seem to have read only other textbooks.

He then posed the question: How can we bridge the gap between the personal and impersonal? *Must* they be kept separate? "What is going on inside pupils when they are given a frog to dissect, or stop to admire the bright blue inside a test tube, or are moved by a moment of history?" English teachers presumably like to encourage their students to brighten their expository themes by introducing a personal note, but they may be troubled by the knowledge that in most other classes and in the great professional world students are usually expected to write impersonally. Today, I should add, they may themselves have suffered in education courses from the influence of "scientific" language, in which all traces of emotion, sensuous appeal, and personality are supposed to be eliminated. Rosen barely indicated in passing a peculiarly modern problem—the flood of barbarous jargon in the social and behavioral sciences, which in government has its counterpart in officialese or gobbledygook, and in business such habits as asking, "What is your reaction to this?" instead of, "What do you think about this?" A possible reason why the seminar passed over this problem is that the profession itself has taken to technical jargon in its writings about education.[1] In any case I suppose English teachers alone cannot be expected to preserve a decent respect for the language. But I would have welcomed a statement that one of their responsibilities today is to combat this epidemic of jargon among educated people, one of the worst diseases of language in the history of literacy.

---

[1] I was a little depressed by the constant references during the seminar to areas, levels, dimensions, patterns, processes—developmental, educative, etc. The profession also seems to be taking over "reaction" as a substitute for "opinion." As I have written elsewhere, I am irritated by this word because it suggests to me what happens when a frog's leg is stimulated by an electric needle, and happens just as well if the frog is decapitated or unconscious.

Another question the seminar did not go into was what special attention, if any, should be given to students preparing to specialize in science or technology. Their kind are the creators of power in modern society, in this respect its rulers, and certainly far more influential than specialists in literature. It might therefore be better not to cater to their technical interests but try all the harder to inculcate the humanistic values of English. Or it might be advisable to encourage them to write scientific or technical exposition, assist them to write it more clearly and effectively for an audience of classmates with diverse interests, instead of swelling the endless complaint that we don't speak the same language; as it is, industry has to employ many men to translate the reports of technicians into clear English. In either case students should know that the language of scientists is not actually uniform or invariably impersonal, but varied to suit their audience—fellow scientists, students, or laymen. It is of course possible to write lucidly, imaginatively, even eloquently about science for the general public, as British scientists in particular have shown, beginning with Thomas Huxley. (Their performance suggests that the traditional training in British schools has been somewhat better than one might gather at the seminar.) And in any case students of science should know that good exposition is not "simple prose," easy to write. Witness Charles Darwin: "I never study style; all that I do is try to get the subject as clear as I can in my head, and express it in the commonest language which occurs to me. But I generally have to think a good deal before the simplest arrangement occurs to me."

Harold Rosen's paper ended, as it began, with large questions: "Could we agree that it is time we formulated a policy on the use of language across the whole curriculum? Could we take the first steps in opening discussions with teachers of other subjects and with other interested parties? Is there any hope of convincing all teachers that the personal response is relevant at all stages?" On the last question the seminar at least implied that there was some hope by its emphatic declarations on the importance of the personal response. It did not, however, explicitly open discussions with teachers of other subjects, beyond indicating a wish that they would cooperate in the teaching of writing. I assume that this neglect was not deliberate, since I got little impression of hostility to science or any other subject; and always the seminar had plenty on its hands in the problems of English proper. But the emphasis on the personal response did distract attention from such broader considerations, and from the need as well of the impersonal response.

Early in the proceedings Wayne Booth pointed to this when he proposed rhetoric as the intellectual center the English curriculum needed if it were to have the "philosophy" the seminar was seeking. In deploring the prevailing tendency to minimize the need of systematic knowledge, the value of techniques of analysis, the pleasures and excitements of "cognition," or in general the importance of *thinking*, he added that a well-educated student in English should be able to read well not only imaginative literature but historical and philosophical works, and to write effectively about them. I would add that in the modern world he ought to have some grasp as well of the fundamentals of science, a lack of which it was sometimes possible to detect in the discussions. In college the major in English ought to learn something about the history, logic, and philosophy of science, if only to get a clearer idea of the values, the limitations, and the abuses of scientific language—and also of the uses and abuses of poetic language.

In staying close to home the seminar did have much to say, however, about another matter neglected in the schools —the teaching of speech, or more strictly talking. One reason for this odd neglect is precisely that man is above all a talking animal, not by nature a writing one. He begins talking in infancy without teaching, through speech learning to adapt himself to adult ways, but he has to be taught to write, just as the race acquired the habit of writing very late in its history; and for many people the habit remains unnatural. In both British and American elementary schools, at any rate, talking is seldom taught except for the inevitable correction of mistakes. In high schools it is taught to some extent under the name of "speech," but it is then usually distinguished from English, given in a separate course taught by speech teachers, and not required of all students. Basil Bernstein, a visiting British sociologist, pointed out a stranger neglect in his science: though there has been much study of socialization, no empirical study has systematically examined the role of speech in the child's acquisition of a "specific *social* identity." (He is himself now investigating such matters as the differences that social class makes in the speech of children.) And the neglect of talking by the schools has become stranger in the modern world, where people are listening to more talk than ever before in history, on radio and television, and many are doing more talking too in the endless committees and conferences alike in business, government, and the professional world. In the democracies, which make so much of free speech, the torrent of platitudinous, illogical, often irresponsible talk, and its acceptance by lazy, uncritical listeners, are provoking books of alarm.[2]

To be sure, the relatively new subject called "speech" has spread rapidly in America. The first M.A. in the subject was granted in 1902, the first Ph.D. as late as 1922, but American universities have by now granted more than 20,000 advanced degrees in it. With this modernization the teaching of the subject has moved away from what some of us knew in our youth as "elocution"; it is now centered on "communication," not performance. It is still primarily a high school subject, however, not taking care of the needs of

---

[2] A recent one is *The Ill-Spoken Word: The Decline of Speech in America,* by Leonard A. Stevens (New York: McGraw-Hill Book Company, 1966).

young children. It is also concerned chiefly with the more formal or public kinds of speech. In listing the qualifications of a competent teacher, the Speech Association of America included such duties as teaching debate, public speaking, and dramatic production, directing speech contests and festivals and theater, radio, and television production, and preparing programs for assemblies, community ceremonies, and special occasions. The seminar was more interested in informal talk in the classroom—conversation or discussion. And its main concern was as usual not a mere "communication skill," but the personal development of children—*all* children, whether or not they have any special interest in acting, debating, or public speaking.

Now, there is no doubt much talk in the ordinary English classroom, and except under the most routine drillmasters, some discussion. But the discussion is seldom a group discussion, or much like a normal conversation. The teacher presides over it from his desk; the youngsters talk to him, not to one another; and all are concerned mainly with getting the right answer. As James Moffett complained, "Most of the furious flagging of hands and clamorous talking at once in traditional classes is actually provoked by the teacher, who usually has asked a question to which he knows the answer. The children are competitively bidding for the teacher's approval and place no value on what other children say." What Moffett and others called for is a democratic group discussion in which the teacher drops "this parental role as dispenser of rewards and punishments." Study groups proposed a deliberate, continuous program of informal talk. I almost said "systematic"; but it was generally agreed that the program should not be built on drills or explicit practice in forms of speech, at least with younger students. The teacher should likewise avoid stress on correct pronunciation and good "delivery" that would make the youngsters self-conscious and discourage their talking freely.

The teacher's immediate role in such a program is to

provide opportunities and plan situations for informal conversation and discussion, often in small groups. In the early
grades he has to lead the discussion, but as the children grow
up he should encourage them to take over the lead. One report declared that the primary school program should create
"virtually unlimited opportunities" for such talk. These need
not all be planned, but may grow out of the spontaneous interests of the group. Reading and writing offer obvious occasions for discussion, which may in turn then enliven the study
of literature and composition. An American contributor who
translated the program into the technical language of educationists suggested that the teacher could work in some
discipline too. While granting that "motivation must be at
an optimum," he added, "Opportunities for using language
are not sufficient for optimum growth in oral proficiency and
power," and "Instruction encouraging proficiency need not
be adverse to development." The seminar seemed more impressed, however, by a rationale suggested by James Moffett.
This began with a systematic "structure of discourse," including rhetoric, that the British could nevertheless welcome
because he built it in personal, dramatic terms.

Since the elements of discourse are a first, second, and
third person—speaker, listener, and subject—Moffett suggested that the starting point in teaching discourse is
"drama": the interaction between the persons. He was interested particularly in dramatic improvisation, but he also
suggested that the class workshop discussion should be a
fundamental activity from kindergarten all the way through
college. Through dialogue youngsters move from face-to-
face drama to narrative, exposition, argument, theory—the
domains of writing. They learn to sharpen, qualify, and
elaborate their thought, without benefit of textbooks. The
teacher should try to create "kinds of dialogue in which
questioning, qualifying, and collaborating are habitual give-
and-take operations." His special art is "to play a dialogue
by ear and exploit the unforeseen twists and turns of it to

explore all those things that textbooks ineffectually try to present to students in an exposition"—rhetoric, style, logic, semantics, etc. If this would seem to be a large order, Moffett's basic requirements for group discussion are simpler. The teacher should lay down the ground rules: no raising of hands, but no interrupting either. He should see to it that the students talk to one another, not just to impress him. He can arrange panel discussions in order to promote "the social art of conversing and the intellectual art of qualifying." Such discussions Moffett much prefers to the prepared speeches of formal debate, "a game of one-upmanship" in which the object is to win, not to enlarge the mind. Group or panel discussions will naturally involve some controversy, but they can do much more to promote "multiplicity, fertility, choice"—the democratic principle of the open market of ideas. In these discussions he sees another argument for heterogeneous classes, which can provide a richer variety in dialect, vocabulary, point of view, and ideas.

Talk, wrote James Britton, is "the sea on which everything else floats." In his paper on the structure of discourse, Moffett summed up by stressing the relations between talk and everything else in the English curriculum:

> I have suggested structuring the English curriculum according to the relations of speaker-listener-subject as the ultimate context within which all our other concerns may be handled functionally and holistically, moving the student in his writing and reading from one kind of actual discourse to the next in a sequence which permits him to learn style, logic, semantics, rhetoric, and literary form continuously through practice as first or second person. . . . The structure of the subject must be meshed with the structure of the student. A major failure of education has been to consider the logic of the one almost to the exclusion of the psychologic of the other. . . .
>
> This paper is a plea to bring the methods of teaching English as nearly in line as possible with the goals—think-

ing, speaking, listening, reading, and writing. This is best done, I claim, not by imitating empirical subjects and asking students to read about writing and write about reading, but by asking them to practice the skills themselves with actual raw materials and audiences, continuously but variously, at all ranges of the symbolic spectrum and in all relations that might obtain between speaker, spoken-to, and spoken-about.

This plea included the means to another neglected end that the seminar endorsed, but did not discuss at length—not only reading, writing, and talking well, but listening well. It is understandable that little was said about how to teach listening: I cannot imagine a course in the subject. If there might be systematic exercises to foster and test ability to listen alertly, closely, the temper of the seminar precluded faith in such a program. The consensus was that in most classes students have had to listen too much as it is. But in a program of informal group discussion they would at least be likely to listen better to both their classmates and the teacher. If some older students tend to find their classmates boring, one reason is the arrested development of most in the talking they have been doing ever since the cradle. As they mature they continue to ramble, but too often grow more halting, obscure, trite, and dull. There is certainly no way of making them all sprightly talkers and eager listeners, but I know of no better way of trying than the continuous program suggested at the seminar.

One more important question on which it agreed without discussion might concern the general public more than it appears to. In arguing for the importance of courses in speech, Jeffery Auer concluded: "Free men, employing free speech, and trained in its effective and ethical use, have always been best equipped to deal with the problems of their day." I would italicize the word *ethical*. It appeared in another statement of the aims of both composition and speech: a recognition that "the use of language, like any other social

111

act, entails an ethical obligation to speak and write respon-
sibly." The common disrespect for this obligation in an age
of high-powered advertising, publicity, and propaganda,
coupled with the as common insensitivity of listeners and
readers to irresponsible uses of language, helps to explain
the doubts whether most free`men are well equipped to
deal with the problems of our day. English teachers can
never be expected to eradicate such abuses of language, but
I would place some effort to combat them high on the list of
their proper aims. They might include among the ideals of
"communication" a saying of Aristotle: "When truth and
falsehood are presented with equal skill, truth will always
prevail." Or since anyone may ask who knows the truth
about our problems, they might ponder a modest suggestion.
Walter Loban, who for years has studied the development
of speech in a group of several hundred children, reports
one finding: "Those subjects who proved to have the greatest power over language . . . were the subjects who most
frequently used language to express tentativeness"—condi-
tioned statements, supposition, hypothesis. Such tentativeness would be fostered better by informal conversation and
discussion in the classroom than by either formal debating
of either-or propositions or encouraging youngsters to wave
hands and give teacher the right answer.

It might also justify a certain inconclusiveness in the
seminar's discussions of how to teach the fundamentals of
composition, as of literature and language.

CHAPTER SEVEN

CREATIVITY AND DRAMA

"Creative" has entered the large company of magic words in America. Businessmen have grown especially fond of it; junior executives and advertising men are alike exhorted to be creative. The ad writers in turn exploit its glamour in selling the public their wares, such as do-it-yourself hobbies and manuals of popular psychology. Even in government one hears of "creative federalism." As all this suggests, however, the rage for creativity has been pretty superficial. Another giveaway is the teaching of English in America: except in the early grades, creative writing gets little attention in either schools or colleges. It is not considered practical, which means that it is unimportant. Writing stories and poems may be all right for the few who like to do such things, but most students—and parents—ask: Where does it get you? Poetry in particular is a dead language for most.

115

Businessmen would be the last to think that poetry is anything but a frill, a waste of time if taken seriously; they take for granted that "normal" boys are not interested in writing it. The "individualism" they pride themselves on is rather different from the individuality fostered by creative writing.

Creativity was a major topic at the seminar because many British schools make much more of it all through their curriculum. In an introductory paper David Holbrook argued that it is no incidental concern, but should be the very "basis of our approach to English teaching as an art"; nothing is more important than developing the child's capacity to explore and express his inner world, realize his personal identity. In a study group that took up the topic, Holbrook and Geoffrey Summerfield backed up their claims by striking examples of the creative work they had elicited from British youngsters. American members of the group were at first disposed to be skeptical, pointing out the need of gifted teachers and the practical necessity of teaching functional prose, but eventually they were convinced that creative writing should be made an essential part of the English curriculum. The British admitted that it was not actually the core of their curriculum, taking up only a period or so a week, and that functional writing of course had to be taught too. In drawing up a comprehensive, detailed program to support their recommendations, they accepted some practical suggestions by Americans. With a caveat or so, the group arrived at an unusually enthusiastic agreement on the importance of creative writing. The seminar as a whole warmly endorsed its report. The topic of creativity provided about the best concrete example of how the two countries could learn from one another.

Now, just because I incline to agree that the schools should do more with it I would first point to the usual complications. "Creativity" is hardly a precise term. The group was unable to agree on a definition of it or on a list of its distinctive characteristics, which included terms no more precise—imaginative, expressive, spontaneous, unpredictable, unique, etc. Sometimes it seemed to mean only "personal" writing, which is common enough in the schools and can be as stereotyped or strictly uncreative as any other kind of writing. The essential problem, David Holbrook wrote, is to know when children are being sincere, "real," or really involved in their writing; but sincerity is no guarantee of imaginative or literary merit. "Creative" is also a misleading term for the same reason that writers and artists have welcomed it as a means of asserting their importance in a world dominated by science and technology. By now it may obscure the plain truth that creative imagination is at work in science and technology too. With youngsters learning to read, write, and think it may be exercised in using "impersonal" language, conveying all kinds of ideas, or trying to make sense of the world. When pressed, Holbrook and Summerfield both granted readily that creativity does not mean merely writing little stories and poems, but may pervade all the interests and activities of children, and ideally should pervade the whole school curriculum. Its ideal outcome is "creative living." I would venture that English professors are no more distinguished for this than natural scientists.

Meanwhile the chief danger in the schools is that to ordinary teachers "creative" means the conventionally literary or "poetic"—prettiness, fluffiness, fanciness. It may even mean the gush of a new magazine of children's writings that a few years ago promised to bring "every season another green fresh draught from that mystic fount of excitement, that depthless well of longing." Textbooks confirm the common addiction to literary embellishment and the purple passage. (One popular manual in America is entitled *Sparkling Words*.) Exercises in creative writing then become another assignment that may oppress youngsters, especially the diffident ones. Bright youngsters are apt to trot out stock responses, since they naturally adopt the literary

postures of their parents and teachers. The inability of many
teachers to recognize the "real thing" may be illustrated by
two samples of children's poetry submitted by Dorothy
Saunders, taken from an article by Herbert Kohl.[1]

Shop with Mom

I love to shop with mom
And talk to the friendly grocer,
And help her make the list
Seems to make us closer.

The Junkies

When they are
in the street
they pass it
along to each
other but when
they see the
police they would
run some would
just stand still
and be beat
so pity ful
that they want
to cry.

Both poems were written by eleven-year-old girls. Kohl
reported that the first poem won high praise and was published in the school paper; the teacher of this girl liked especially its pleasant, wholesome sentiment and the rhyme
"closer" and "grocer." The second poem, much more poi-
gnant, was not published. The teacher who edited the school
paper complained that it was marred by some mistakes in

---

[1] His article was later published in the *New York Review of Books*
(November 17, 1966). I am indebted to him for permission to reprint the
samples and the gist of his comment on them.

English, it had no rhyme or meter, and it was not really poetry at all. In particular she was horrified by the subject, saying that the little girl couldn't possibly know what junkies were, and the other children would never be interested in such a poem. So the teacher's pathetic devotion to propriety kept her both insensitive to poetry and ignorant of children, not to say of life.

Some samples of children's poetry presented by Sybil Marshall raised more difficult questions. The seminar discussed at some length the following three poems on wishing:

> I wish I were a little bird
> To skim the sky and be unheard
> To watch the people down below
> The farmer with his rake and hoe
> What is it like to sleep in a tree
> With leaves and breeze and sky and me?

> If I had a wish
> I'd wish to be a fish
> But then I might wish
> Against all other fish.
> Oh! Then I'd wish
> To be a gull
> And eat the fish
> Till I was full.

> I wish I liked onions.
> They have a penetrating smell.
> On a plate they look delicious
> Small, curly, like small snails
> In the pan, crisling away
> Oh! I do hope that one day
> I get to like onions.

About the first poem there was general agreement: this boy was just going through the assigned motions of making a poem. (The only reason he wished to "be unheard" was that this rhymed with "bird.") The second poem, however, provoked considerable disagreement. Some thought that this too was a synthetic performance. Others thought that it was a genuine, if fumbling, effort by a boy who was at least exploring his experience; they were impressed by his unconventional idea of "wishing against." The suggestion of aggressiveness in his wish to be a gull also impressed one Britisher whose eyes lighted up whenever he made out a revelation of hatred, preferably unconscious (Ha! this must be creative); he judged the poem to be an interesting failure. Most appeared to agree with a comment that the poem could not be judged fairly without some knowledge of the author and his circumstances: it might be a careless, lazy effort by a bright boy, or a promising effort by a boy only beginning to learn how to express himself. I thought this uncertainty might have raised more question about the value of creative writing, especially since I gathered that even in England teachers expect mostly so-so performances; that this poem might have been quite "sincere" made it no better. The conflicting or suspended judgment also pointed to a serious difficulty in instituting a large-scale program of creative writing. The possible value of such writing can be realized only if students get considerable individual attention from sensitive, sympathetic, imaginative teachers.

Still, there remains the poem about onions. Nobody questioned that it was fresh and genuine; this youngster (I suppose a girl) had her eye and her mind on her subject. Such performances are at least common enough to make a good case for creative writing. To approach this case, I cite another sample offered by David Holbrook—pieces about fire by thirteen-year-olds. One poem that had flames leaping high and sparkling on the lea was left unfinished by the boy, apparently aware that he was going nowhere. Another began promisingly with "Sir Fire is a creeping thing, a crawling thing, a weeping thing," but petered out in romance and history about cavemen. (Its author appended a postscript: "I'm sorry if this pome seems short but to me it's full.") Then came this prose poem, which may speak for itself:

Fire is not understanding; he is reckless and ruthless. He bites when you touch him, he is angry. Why? Who has upset him? Why does he roar when devouring one thing and purr when devouring another? He is a giver of heat but he doesn't want you to take it. The naked tongues of flame reach high into the sky as if searching for food.

He hates the wind and the rain, the wind makes him curl up and hide and the rain makes him spit in a fury of rain and smoke.

What makes him so reckless? Why does he find pleasure in destroying things? Why does he gnash his teeth in anger at metallic objects? He is so powerful, he stops at nothing!

What would we do without fire? He gives us our power, he cooks our food, he is our angry helper!

American adolescents, deep in grammar or sentence exercises, might be baffled by this piece, or might be awed by it. In either case they are likely to say what many college freshmen say about their difficulties in composition: "I don't have enough imagination," or "I can't seem to get an inspiration." Dorothy Saunders and Sybil Marshall would answer that their imagination has been smothered by their schooling. Both insisted that youngsters entering school do not instinctively resist learning to write, but have a natural love for playing with words, inventing stories, entertaining their classmates in a make-believe world, often one of gay nonsense and adventure in which the child-hero shows up the stupid adults. In their eagerness they as naturally develop some sense of form and appropriateness in style. What they resist is mechanical exercises and set assignments, any suggestion of "Now sit down, shut up, and write a poem." The teacher's job is to get them started by providing suggestive

121

experiences—not stock subjects like spring—through pictures, poems, stories, or class situations. She should keep them feeling free by encouraging them, pointing out only what is good in their work, not dwelling on their errors or shortcomings. Criticism should come gradually and tactfully at a later stage.

In American schools the teaching of creative writing usually stops abruptly at about the fifth grade. Then students are given conventional assignments in exposition and drills in mechanics—and they begin to rebel against writing. In the many British schools where they continue with creative or personal writing they may profit more from it as they mature. David Holbrook sees its primary value in all that the student learns about himself as he explores the mysteries, wonders, and terrors of the inner world—exemplified by the vivid prose poem on fire, which may reflect the problems of adolescence. With such growth in personality, students also grow more sensitive to the world about them, more alert and perceptive. They may better exercise their powers of choice and enjoy more real freedom of choice. They may better resist all the tendencies to mechanization, standardization, and regimentation that deaden sensibility, all the pressures to conformism that stunt or stifle individuality. For such reasons Holbrook is pleased to believe that an imaginative program of creative writing is far from mush —it is dynamite. The seminar agreed that it was particularly important as a means of combatting the inhuman trends in modern civilization.

On a philosophical level, to which Holbrook referred, Suzanne Langer has illumined the sources of creativity by pointing out that a primary need of man is the need of symbolizing. Man is distinctively a symbol-making animal. He is forever engaged in the process because unlike other animals he communicates by the symbolism of language and lives in a cultural world of symbols, which form his thoughts and feelings about nature, his fellows, and himself. Scientists have explained and mastered the physical world by a set of symbols that have grown quite respectable, even though nobody ever sees what they call an electron. The symbols by which poets and artists express the inner world of feeling and fantasy are less precise, more suggestive, and often unconscious, sprung from the deep sources of our being, and today they seem more obviously fictitious. The scientifically minded tend to disparage the inner world as merely "subjective," implying "unreal" or at best a lower grade of reality than the external, objective world; whereas to the individual nothing is more real. If what the youngster managed to say about fire in his prose poem is scientifically untrue, and less useful than what chemists say about it, it is nevertheless meaningful and humanly important. To the practical question of where this kind of writing gets you, a sufficient answer is that it may make you more alive, give you a more interesting self to live with, or simply get you the satisfaction of having *made* something really your own.

To elicit such writing, Holbrook and Summerfield use much the same methods. They try to avoid fixed assignments and the kind of predictability that oppresses the ordinary student of composition, the knowledge that he will have to do some writing every Wednesday at ten o'clock. They recommended "loosening up" exercises, often by a kind of free association, using music, passages of prose or poetry, paintings, or other modes of creativity. Summerfield illustrated by an elaborate stage he once set up to stimulate a class of ten- or eleven-year-olds. He began with a study of medieval Peking, recreating its life with the help of Chinese poems, paintings, screens, and the like. Among other things the children made dragon kites before they settled down to writing poems. The outcome was a set of unusually successful poems, which they gathered into a book with illustrations. Here is an example:

The Earth-Dragon Erupts

The Earth-Dragon is red and fiery,
Smoke comes belching out of his nostrils
His body glows hot and his eyes flash fire
Lava races livid along his veins
He is a raging fury and ready to erupt.
From the depths of his mountain comes
An ominous rumbling
And people out of their beds come tumbling
To rush to the Earth-Dragon's temple.

The dragon is not pleased with their meagre off'ring
So, thundering from the mountain
Comes a river of lava
To wipe out the occupants of the town
To Kingdom come!
And, in the space of five minutes,
Some people of the town pass
From sleep to eternity
Without even knowing it.

At that the children were not required to write poems, but were left free to choose some other creative activity, such as painting, making bamboo screens, or building junks. Like Holbrook, Summerfield believes in encouraging children by giving them their head as much as possible. As for the problem of what to do with the many who come up with poor work, their answer was to play it gently by ear. First the teacher of creative writing must try to know his different students and win their trust by showing a sympathetic interest in all their efforts.

The British then had to meet the obvious criticism they were liable to, that they were letting down the bars, neglecting the necessary discipline. They answered that their students were not simply indulging themselves or having a gay time, but typically were intent, purposeful, and uncommonly busy, since creative writing is not at all easy work. Thus the

124

children who got engrossed in medieval Peking listened and read closely, worked harder on their poems, while they were also learning something about a different way of life. And the poems of these children brought up a practical argument in support of creative writing. An American marveled because some of them contained semicolons—a stylistic feat many college freshmen are not up to. They might shame the freshmen by their vocabulary too, and their freedom from awkwardness. For once youngsters get really interested in their writing they naturally try to improve it, and may write more maturely than others who are merely carrying out assignments. They may likewise take more pains to avoid errors and do a workmanlike job. The argument is that creative or personal writing is an excellent way, perhaps the best way, to improve the basic skills of writing and achieve a mastery of language.

Although there is some evidence indicating that students so trained wrote more correctly as well as effectively than others who had been drilled in mechanics, I would again not have high hopes that extensive research could prove much about this argument. Too much would depend on such immeasurables as the quality of the teachers and the depth of the interest they aroused. We cannot be sure either that skill in creative or personal writing necessarily leads to skill in writing for practical purposes, such as scientific exposition; it might make this all the more boring to students. But assuming that a student has got really interested in expressing himself, it seems reasonable to assume that some connection with functional writing is likely. He at least has developed an interest in writing lacking in too many students who have been forced to write much "practical" prose about matters not close to their experience, for them not actually very practical because not meaningful. He may appreciate that good expository writing is creative too. His training will have limbered up not only his imagination but his sensibility, his powers of perception. Holbrook stressed in particular his openness to experience, in which thinking begins. He is less likely to write a stilted, stereotyped prose, or to succumb to the jargon that passes for English in so much technical writing. Clear writing can be a cause as well as an effect of clear thinking. Practical, hard-headed men need to be reminded that good creative writing is a product of thought and hard work, not merely of imagination.

With literature the connections are much plainer. As one way of stimulating creative writing is reading poems and stories, so the experience of this writing helps young-sters to read more sensitively and appreciatively. It opens doors and windows on both life and literature, gives them insights into both. Having written a poem, they may be shown how an adult poet treated a similar experience or problem. (Blake and D. H. Lawrence are favorites with the British for such purposes.) Although these connections with literature have yet to be thoroughly explored or conclusively proved, I assume no one would question that creative writ-ing is likely to improve skills in reading, stimulate a desire to read, and heighten pleasure in literature.

Yet all finally depends upon the teacher; so we are brought back to the practical difficulties. Very few English teachers have been trained to teach creative writing; a great many have been unfitted for it by their training. Manuals are least helpful for such purposes; creativity might be described as antitextbook. Holbrook and Summerfield met the problem by including in their summary report detailed recommenda-tions for a teacher preparation program. To teach creative work well requires a "very exacting training," which they proved by the qualifications they specified. Among other things, teachers need to know a wide range of literature, to have high standards of appreciation, and to have a feeling for excellence in writing; they need the experience of cre-ativity in some form so that they may know what it is like for their students; they need to know children well and to have made close studies of their writing; they need to have high standards in practical expression too; and they need "to be confident enough to tolerate silence, failure, slow development, and confused or hesitant expressions." Ordinary mortals preparing to teach English might be dismayed by these requirements.

A caveat to the consensus of the study group pointed to further difficulties. Reed Whittemore, himself a poet and a teacher of creative writing in an American college, warned against the tendency to take a narrow view of creativity, a cloudy name for processes that we know very little about, and to fall into a kind of arrogance. The authors of the group's report had declared, for example, that one aim was to "break the clichés that stand between the child and the full range of his experience." Whittemore commented: "Yet any teacher who attempts to fulfill that aim in class will be logically bound to go against his own instructions—that is, he will be bound to prescribe a *limit* to the range of the child's experience by discouraging him from recording that part of his experience which *is* cliché (or, in psychological jargon, by failing to reinforce him when he demonstrates a passion for cliché)." The child may well have to live with his clichés, let us add, and need them for his security. The devotees of creativity were also making rather heavy demands on him when they included among its distinctive characteristics the "unique" response.

Implicitly they called attention to another problem when they declared that they did not oblige all their students to write poems or stories—the problem of the many who do not take to creative writing because of shyness, backwardness, sullenness, or whatever reason. To be sure, they reported with some striking evidence that much can be done with children of low IQ's too. But even when they stressed that young children are naturally fond of writing, they admitted under question that some are not very eager or fluent. Always they have to deal with the many poor efforts—the reason why teachers of creative writing need to be able to tolerate "silence, failure," etc. And with older children teachers have to deal with the problem of the many who in fact have little imagination, no flair for writing, whether or not because of their schooling. It might seem inhuman to require of them efforts at creativity that they know are far inferior to the efforts of some classmates. They may have to sweat through even simple personal writing.[2] Consider as well all the teachers who dote on "literary" effects, the manuals that lay out exercises in personification and simile, and I conclude that there is little hope that in America much more will be done with creative writing for some time.

For the long run, however, I would conclude on a note of hope. Despite its vagueness, "creativity" is not a meaningless word, any more than "imagination" is; both can be recognized and widely agreed upon in the greater works alike in the arts and sciences, and in the better efforts of children. British teachers have demonstrated the exciting possibilities of creative writing in the schools and are beginning to train teachers to follow them. (David Holbrook has taught in a summer institute for teachers in America.) American schools are doing more in the early grades and may begin to do more in the upper ones, now that universities are taking up the practice of having a creative writer in residence, others on the faculty of English departments. A real start has been made in both countries. And if the recommendations of the specialists in creativity have a utopian air, this may again help more than would modest proposals for immediate changes. In so far as the news gets around, it might attract more bright, eager young people into the teaching of English.

---

[2] I write with some feeling as one who in his youth read too many hundreds of freshman themes about travels that were supposedly broadening, sports that built character, and so on and on, and who had somehow to parry questions from too many students who wanted a B but were going at top speed when they made C.

And so with the proposals of another mixed study group that concentrated on the related topic of "drama"—creative activities quite different from the familiar reading and producing of plays. They begin with mime or pantomime and improvisation, the enacting of homemade dramas in the classroom. The contents of the drama may be known stories, drawn from fairy tales, children's books, or television, or they may be made up from the children's experience, as in improvising on domestic and other familiar situations. Older children begin writing scripts for them. These performances are not staged for parents or others, but simply for the sake of the children's own education; there is no "playing to an audience." Such activities are carried on in the early grades in both countries, but in America they stop early; the British believe they should be continued throughout the school years. Any Americans in the study group who thought otherwise were quickly converted. No other group reached such complete agreement so soon on their basic recommendations to the seminar—here, that drama in this sense be made an integral part of the English curriculum from beginning to end.

Their initial argument was that such activities capitalize on the drama implicit in the nature of the classroom, the interplay between the teacher and the class and between the diverse members of the class. In making the classroom an ensemble, they liberate students from the constraints of self-consciousness; they can be especially helpful to students with low IQ's or limited vocabulary, and so constitute another argument for heterogeneous classes. Above all, they realize the rich potentialities of drama—a primal activity, rooted in the ritual and play going far back in man's history, and in the dramatic play of children on their own. Today this is especially valuable as a supplement and corrective of an education that is predominantly verbal; the students learn by doing instead of merely reading about it. At the same time, they develop skills in the use of language, since they are both creators and actors of the drama. It is another means of developing and expressing creativity. And perhaps more than creative writing it widens and deepens the students' understanding of life and themselves as they improvise and act various roles, speak in both their own voice and the voice of others. Benjamin DeMott, the most enthusiastic of the American converts, emphasized that drama brought the stuff of life into the English classroom—the life of feeling, in all the variousness that textbooks reduce to academic order. Students may learn the first principle of good writing: "What we truly have in good writing is a moment-to-moment embodiment of the breathing contradictoriness of a living mind: we are given vouchers of variousness."

James Moffett spelled out most fully such connections with composition and literature in a long chapter on drama, of which I can here give only a sketchy account. The first movement away from dialogue is monologue, the sustained, connected speech; it is the natural pathway to other forms of discourse and to writing. Another pathway is rhetoric, for the study of which Moffett believes drama is the perfect place to begin. Rhetoric as he conceives it "refers to the ways one person attempts to act on another, to make him laugh or think, squirm or thrill, hate or mate." By mere crying the infant begins learning "the tremendously important art of manipulating other people," and once he begins to speak he is bound to employ something like rhetoric, however crude or unconscious. Leading students through all such connections with everyday discourse, Moffett would eventually have them write plays—not to make potential dramatists out of them, but to further their education in English. "A student who writes a play is learning how to converse, to appreciate an art form, to understand himself, to describe, and, very generally, simply to write."

British teachers added concrete illustrations from their experience. Anthony Adams reported how a teacher may build up a situation, say a street scene on a busy Saturday night. After some talk about all that goes on, the children choose and act various roles—shopkeepers and peddlers, a family on a stroll, the policeman on his beat, and so forth. Then the teacher may suddenly inject a bit of drama, news that a stone has been thrown through a shop window: *how do they respond?* The children try to do so appropriately. All this can be played out in pantomime or in words; Adams' policy is to begin with pantomime, as a valuable discipline, and let the speech come when it develops naturally out of the situation. Following the drama, some discussion of it suggests writing assignments: character sketches, descriptions of what they saw and did, accounts from contrasting points of view, as of the policeman and a small boy in the crowd. These may draw on supplementary readings and on observations of the happenings in the main street on Saturday. Out of all this may come a little book, to which each child has contributed according to his interests and abilities.

With older children the drama assignments naturally grow more elaborate. Adams had a tenth grade class do a project based on the seven deadly sins, splitting up into seven groups, with some competition for the more interesting sins; from this he led them into Molière.[3] Douglas Barnes told of presenting scripts of plays to re-create. He had a class of thirteen-year-olds improvise in pairs a squabble between a man and his supercilious wife who leaves in a huff, act alone a mixture of fear and determination in approaching a growling dog, fondle and talk to it, and act out other situations similar to those in the prologue of George Bernard Shaw's *Androcles and the Lion.* Finally they acted the whole prologue in groups, enlivening it with their own perceptions.

---

[3] He also introduced some material on the history of the theater, and so was momentarily embarrassed when an American reminded him that the British frowned on such "knowledge." He explained that he merely filtered in some knowledge. My notion is that all the good British teachers work in more knowledge than they may care to admit, but in ways that should allay their worries about its fatal effects.

In this way they are led to the appreciation of whole plays. Barnes believes that the talk of a group engaged in interpreting a script may be the most meaningful form of literary criticism for most of them.

This whole approach to English seems to me not only much more imaginative but more fruitful than what goes on in most of our classrooms. Subscribing to the consensus, I therefore bring up conscientiously the tiresome complications. One was suggested by a British teacher who has seen students "blossom or shrink" in dramatic activities—and who when a student himself had done nothing but shrink. Some children are reluctant to step out and try new roles because they feel isolated or insecure; so we risk doing them serious harm. "The deprived child and the child with the minority accent will be rejected yet again (or confined to comic or class-defined roles which will limit, not extend his conception of the roles open to him in life). The boy with the breaking voice or the clumsy manner will once again be laughed at, rather than laughed with." Older children who have decided on their role in life—say the impersonality of the scientific style—may not want to risk their security by joining in drama, and if forced to do so will probably fail to enter the part anyway. Especially for the British, so much concerned about the development of children as individuals, it would seem that the students ought to have the right to refuse to join in. As it is, improvisation "strengthens the self-assertive and weakens the insecure."

The study group recognized this possible danger in their report to the seminar and gave what I assume is the only possible answer: "all education is in this sense a dangerous business." They added that drama was no riskier than the rest of the curriculum, and that in the last resort they would defend the child's right not to take part. I would add that perhaps no subject in the schools is more dangerous than the study of literature, which if it takes at all must have some effect on the student's personality; nor is it at all certain that "good" literature (even D. H. Lawrence—an idol of the British delegation) necessarily has a good effect. The risks spring from the very power and value of imaginative literature. For better or worse, we have finally to depend on the good taste and judgment of the teacher. The one who issued the warning about drama trusted that it would help the teacher to minimize the danger.

Hence we are led back to the usual practical difficulties. Few English teachers in America have been trained to teach such dramatic activities; many might feel as uneasy as the older students if asked to start improvising. The seminar therefore recommended that a team of American teachers be given the opportunity to tour British secondary schools that have a strong program in drama. Assuming that American schools do get interested in experimenting with a similar program (as I would hope), another problem arises. Dramatic activities cannot be carried on in the conventional box classroom with its rows of desks. They require space, movable furniture, rostrums, ideally equipment for making a tape or a book, "publishing" the work done. A large-scale program in drama would require the overhauling of both our schools and the curriculum, at some expense—maybe as much as a fleet of bombers costs. As always the question is: Are school boards, superintendents, lawmakers, taxpayers, and parents willing to support such a program?

CHAPTER EIGHT

THE MASS MEDIA AND MYTH

In view of the initial agreement that English teachers
have been teaching too much that is "not English," it might
seem surprising that the seminar proposed the inclusion of
some study of the mass media in the curriculum, and that
no group protested against the recommendation; but the
agreement was easy to understand. The seminar had in other
respects settled for a broad curriculum, including dramatic
activities, and it had recognized new needs created by modern society. The mass media—moving pictures, radio, television—not only present a great deal of narrative and drama
but typify the "communications revolution" that can hardly
be ignored by teachers of language and literature. They have
a profound influence on the interests, sentiments, attitudes,
and tastes of youngsters whom the teachers are trying to
introduce to literature. They mold the popular or "mass cul-

ture" that is among the most distinctive characteristics of modern society, and another inescapable condition of mass education. And who else in the schools would give attention to this ubiquitous culture if English teachers ignored it? Teachers of "social studies" might be candidates, but they have not been trained in the uses of language and literature.

Somewhat more surprising was the prevailing attitude toward the mass media. It was not mainly hostile even though they are the most powerful competitors of literature today, menacing the once natural habit of reading books for pleasure. To be sure, some participants attacked them for the all too familiar reasons—the trashiness of most of their programs, the exploitation of violence, sex, and sadism, etc. (One launched periodic diatribes against the most popular James Bond.) All were aware of the essential differences between the folk culture of past societies and popular culture today: the one an often coarse but always genuine expression of the thought and feeling of the common people, of and by them; the other a synthetic, commercialized culture manufactured *for* the people by professionals, who always say they are only giving them what they want but generally tend to appeal to the lowest common denominator, often cynically cash in on the worst tastes of people. Nevertheless most participants chose not to treat the mass media as simply the enemy. Some pointed out that mere diatribes did little good; a frontal attack was poor strategy, since they were certainly here to stay. More maintained that the English teacher should try to make the best of them as new art forms and could hope to do so because of the wide range of their offerings, which included reputable works along with all the trash. Those who were repelled by the mass media could agree that the teacher should help youngsters to be less passive in their choices, to reflect on them, and to develop more discriminating tastes in a source of entertainment they were sure to feed on anyway.

For the British this agreement was easier because of

BBC. Their television industry, not dominated by Madison Avenue types, is more responsible than the big American networks, and it offers many more programs serviceable for English teachers. But the Americans voiced no opposition to the agreement. In general, the educators at the seminar were neither cloistered scholars, academic in the depressing sense, nor fastidious literary people, disdainful even of "mid-cult." They did not rehearse the literary clichés about our standardized mass society and culture if only because as educators they knew, once more, that it is also an extraordinarily heterogeneous society. Some warned against the snobbery implicit in disdain of "the masses," meaning "all but us." In particular, all were much concerned about children—the many bright, eager children, the too many poor, handicapped ones, and always the individual child. The child today is subject to the massive pressures to standardization, regimentation, and conformism; but anyone who keeps an eye on him knows that he is not simply a little mass-man.

Now, the seminar did not come out with a comprehensive program for the teaching of the mass media. No one group made this its main topic for study, and none of the groups that considered it offered detailed suggestions about how they should be taught, how much time should be allotted to them, or at what stage—not to mention such practical considerations as the question whether most English teachers are well enough qualified for this job, or could be expected to become so on top of all their other duties. Some matters that seemed to me important were touched on only briefly, if at all. Suggestions acceptable to the seminar implied, however, that use should be made of moving pictures and television all through the school years. One general session was devoted to the use of related technological innovations in the English classroom. In informal discussions speakers now and then referred to the whole problem of modern technology and what it is doing to people—for example, the constant assault on the human senses, which some thought might be best combatted by music and visual education. In this discursive chapter I am gathering together suggestions offered in various connections, and some bearings of still other discussions, as of myth, on the uses and abuses of the mass media.

There was little discussion of a paper centered on the issue, one on the electronic age offered by Harley Parker of Canada. A disciple of Marshall McLuhan, whose recent books *The Gutenberg Galaxy* and *Understanding Media* have been widely publicized, Parker contended that our culture has emphasized "visual orientation" ever since the invention of the printing press, but is now "being reorganized in sensory terms towards the primacy of the audile-tactile." His listeners appeared to have some doubts about his stress on the "tactile," or at least its relevance to the problems of teaching English. They showed more interest in a paper by Benjamin DeMott (a reprint of an article published in *Esquire*), which devastated the claims made by McLuhan. DeMott attacked especially his complacency about our electronic age as "the greatest of all human ages, whether in the arts or the sciences." Thus the new prophet tells us that while opening "the doors of audile-tactile perception to the non-visual world of spoken language and food and the plastic arts," television has transformed "American innocence into depth sophistication, independently of 'content.'" The computer, a potential means of carrying out "orchestrated programming for the sensory life of entire populations," promises "a Pentecostal condition of universal understanding and unity . . . a perpetuity of collective harmony and peace." As for our supposedly pampered children, they are doing their initial bit by working "furiously"—working harder than children ever did in the past—"processing data in an electrically structured world." All this to the tune of ultramodern jargon, such as "interiorization of alphabetic technology."

Father Walter Ong, who takes a kindlier view than DeMott of McLuhan's work, introduced some ideas more clearly relevant to the teaching of English in a talk on the historic changes in the verbal media. Before the invention of the printing press (the rise of "typographical man" discussed in *The Gutenberg Galaxy*), people had been primarily "oral." They lived in the "free-flowing world of oratory and epic"; they thought of knowledge as story, not causal analysis. In the Middle Ages, when manuscripts began to multiply, examinations were still wholly oral, never written. But once words were "locked in space" by the printing press literate people naturally thought more in terms of the visualized word and lived in a more constrained world.[1] Now, too, the mind was conceived as having "contents." In our electronic age, however, people are again becoming more oral. Although not returning to the early stage—as no one brought up on print can—they are making more use of sound and listening to much more talk.

For English teachers the plainest implication of this change is the need of giving more attention to talking and listening. Elsewhere Ong has suggested that the change had something to do with the furore over Webster's latest dictionary. Whereas lexicographers had always looked to writers for their norms, Webster III paid much more attention to spoken language and so brought back something of the old "free-flowing world." Having invested so much psychic energy in the mastery of writing and print, and of the constraints they imposed, many people did not welcome this openness, but resented the threat to the regularities and certainties that bolstered their self-respect. Ong has also noted the value of our electronic culture in again making possible more *personal* communication. I suppose this may have some connection with the cult of "personality" in

---

[1] Father Ong noted incidentally that under severe psychological pressures illiterate peoples rarely retreat into a dream world or become schizophrenic. Their response to intolerable pressures is a sudden burst of anxiety —going berserk or running amok. Readers may reflect on the mixed blessings of literacy.

America—personality conceived as an acquired manner, like that of the people in ads or the celebrities on TV, which can be turned on and off, and which therefore has little to do with genuine individuality, being a real person. In any case it recalls the profound influence of the mass media, about which Father Ong does not share McLuhan's complacence. They are "part of the student's life world," often the chief source of his ideas about life and his values; "and if he cannot see what they do to him—for good or for bad—and recognize his own responsibility for the part they play in his life, he certainly cannot be expected to do anything very real with Shakespeare or Golding or anyone else." English teachers can help him to see this. They may then help him to realize what literature can do for him that the mass media seldom if ever can—not merely arouse but sustain his interest, deeply engage him, and develop his powers of reflection.

In the general preoccupation with the new mass media, the seminar gave little attention to an old one predating the electronic age—the press. Reed Whittemore submitted to a study group some samples of journalistic prose to make a point about the teaching of composition and offset the loose talk about "creativity." They illustrated the practical uses of writing that students should know about, since these take up about ninety percent of the world's writing. (It should be remembered that writing was invented five thousand years ago for practical bookkeeping purposes—not literary ones.) In newspapers such writing is not merely factual but at best imaginative, and even in cliché-ridden passages is likely to be full of animistic metaphors, as on the financial page: "Steadying after Monday's sharp decline, prices edged upward in the first hour of trading but fell back later in the morning." Some samples, however, raised troublesome questions. One was a news item about Red China that exemplified the common practice of coloring and slanting the news, a disguised form of propaganda that most readers are unaware of except for a vague notion that you can't believe everything you read in the papers. Another was a typical passage from *Playboy* that presumably impressed its readers as ultrasophisticated—a tawdry eulogy of the topless bathing suit "in all its undulating, aureate glory," so far confined to the "golden littoral" of California.

The question is: Should this kind of writing be taken up in class in order to make clear to students how irresponsible and degrading it is? Although a brief discussion in the study group was inconclusive, the British seemed inclined to offer students only good writing, hoping thereby to make them sensitive enough to recognize meretricious stuff. I doubted that Americans could afford to be so hopeful, considering the popularity of the meretricious even among college graduates, though this may be due to the failure of the schools to get most students seriously interested in literature. But I thought it more unfortunate that the seminar did not find time to discuss the question raised by the newspapers, which almost all students will continue to read. Would it not be desirable to try to teach them how to read the news, recognize when and how it is slanted and distorted, sometimes suppressed? More broadly, should not some analysis of propaganda be included in the English curriculum?

As it is often said, ours is an age of propaganda. The mass media have made possible infinitely more professional, systematic, high-powered propaganda than in any previous age. The periodic alarm over insidious political or "foreign" propaganda obscures the incessant, ubiquitous, quite respectable propaganda of publicity and advertising. (One thing the big advertising agencies are not good at, incidentally, is books.) One study group did briefly recommend that "for teachers who are interested" the analysis of advertising might be given some time. "It helps students to be more critical of appeals to them as consumers or voters, to use the media rather than be exploited by them, and to be more sensitive in their use of and responses to language of all kinds." No doubt many English teachers are neither interested nor competent in such analysis and would be fearful of taking on so "controversial" a job. It might be added that they have no time to spare for it, English classes cannot do everything, and intelligent reading should be as much the concern of other courses in the humanities. The trouble remains that no other major subject takes on the job; fundamental problems get overlooked in the specialization and division of labor; and as a result most students never do learn to read intelligently in this respect. When adults, too many continue both as consumers and as voters to respond to appeals based on the assumption that they cannot distinguish blah-blah from thought or simple good sense. "Reaction" may be the right word for their behavior.

Herein is my excuse for bringing in at this point an extraneous topic that a study group did focus on—the uses of myth. They were interested primarily in its literary uses, under the broader topic of "translation." Translation from language to language, past to present, distant to near, offers students ways of looking at the world and valuing experience different from their own. Myth carries them back to the oldest sources of poetry, drama, and fiction, the archetypes of human experience in the natural world before it had been explained, or disguised, in terms of abstract knowledge. With the rise of science and industry, more obviously efficient ways of dealing with the natural world, myth came to be regarded as primitive or childish, something to be "exploded." Nevertheless it is deeply embedded in our cultural heritage.

With its outgrowths—folklore, fairy tale, legend, romance—myth was once upon a time part of the common store of knowledge that writers took for granted, but teachers no longer can. (Most allusions to Bible stories, for instance, mean nothing to American students.) Mythology can accordingly give older students a deeper sense of the past and of our common humanity. It is a symbolic expression of elemental and universal realities, the age-old rhythms, the cycle of the seasons, or of life and death and new life out of death, and so the themes of rebirth, resurrection, regeneration—all deeply embedded in religion too. Today the man on the street, living in a mechanized world, has little sense of these deep connections between the life of man and the natural world, or of elemental rhythms and recurrences; but he pays a price for all the comforts and conveniences that enable him to live in a world of man's own making. As Father Ong wrote, "Primitive man banged his drums to attune himself to cosmic harmonies. Modern man resorts to jazz to get away from it all."

With apologies to the group, I shall not go into all they had to say about the importance and value of myth and the problems of teaching it, including the conflicting theories about it. (One member sounded the invariable warning of the British: myth may distract attention from the particular, unique literary work.) Here I shall take up only one theme —that myth, or the mythological mode of thinking, is still very much alive. It is embodied in the countless animistic metaphors of everyday speech, as of journalistic prose. It lurks in the depths of modern literature, beneath the naturalistic surface, in variations on the age-old themes. It appears even in science, as in Freud's myth of the murder of the primordial father that gave birth to the Oedipus complex— what he believed was an actual historical event. Broadly defined, it may be found in all kinds of popular legends and beliefs, since men still have a basic need of giving symbolic form to their deeper hopes, fears, loves, and hates, and in particular to their communal sentiments and beliefs—the social and political myths nations live by. American examples include the myths of the frontier, the manifest destiny of the nation "under God," and the favorite national legend, the success story—the Horatio Alger myth of the poor boy who always makes good.

In this view popular culture today looks more vulgar and trashy, the electronic age not at all like the great age Marshall McLuhan rhapsodizes over in polysyllables. The myths, legends, and fairy tales for adults featured in the entertainment offered by the mass media have one morbid quality in common—they must always have a happy ending. The basic complaint about TV in particular is that its staple product is mush, lacking any ingredients of either honest thought or deep feeling. By contrast, the largely illiterate peoples of the past look much more mature than Americans. Their mythologies are not collections of success stories; their national epics and legends often have tragic endings. Likewise the popular audience that Shakespeare wrote for could still face up to the tragic realities of the human condition, which have been reflected in mythology. Never before have peoples gorged themselves so constantly on pap. The national mania for the happy ending points to a particular problem of the teacher of literature, that for most Americans literature is another means of escaping life, or getting away from it all, not of getting more deeply into it.

But the popular fables also bring up a more complex issue. In their respect for myth, the study group—and the seminar at large—generally agreed with Paul Olson: "The business of the English teacher is not, primarily, to 'demythologize'—whatever the mythology." Let the science teacher be the critic and expose the superstition it may embody. Presumably the English teacher should teach only the great or good myths. If he takes students into the subject at all deeply, however, I should think he ought to face up to a problem concealed by the current fashion of celebrating the "timeless truth" of myth: that many myths—even Greek and Biblical ones—are strictly barbarous, repulsive, and that myth itself provides no criterion for making such discriminations. The devotees of myth may also forget how dangerous it can be today, or how compelling the need of "demythologizing." Many Americans still believe the nasty myth, suggested by Scripture, that God created Negroes inferior to white men.

The plainest, ugliest example of the danger is the racial

146

mythology of Hitler, which justified the extermination in cold blood of six million Jews as well as countless Slavs. The bitterest critic of the mass media used Hitler to clinch his case against them: without them he could never have swayed the German masses as he did. Another speaker then hinted of a further complication. Hitler was supported by most German professors of literature, and his propaganda chief, Goebbels, got a Ph.D. in literature. Nobody mentioned a disagreeable implication, that those who take for granted that the mass media have a bad effect on people too easily assume that serious literature must have good effects. Hitler's mythology had deep roots in German tradition stemming from the romantic movement. I venture the heresy that the Germans might have done no better had they been devotees of D. H. Lawrence, a postromantic. He was no fascist, as some of his critics charged; but he was no lover of democracy either, and in one aspect he had fascist affinities in his primitivism, his worship of instinct and intuition, his scorn of the claims of reason or intellect—a mythological way of thinking that perhaps called for some "demythologizing," even at the risk of making him appear less "unique." For those concerned with the social responsibilities of education, he illustrates the need of teaching literary works—at least to older students—not only as unique works but in context, with some attention to their relation to literary tradition and to the life and thought of their time.[2] A teacher of literature might profit from some knowledge of social as well as literary history and criticism.

Lawrence leads us to the broader subject of modern technology and science—a main source of his hatred of modern civilization, and of the unhappiness of many literary

---

[2] At the seminar none of Lawrence's admirers mentioned one of his characteristic pronouncements: "The great mass of the population should never be taught to read and write. Never." This might be regarded as the ultimate logic of the policy of not intervening in the "natural" development of children.

147

people. In a paper on the new technological aids for English teachers, Alfred Grommon began by mentioning the anxieties of writers over the electronic age, the proliferation of machines like the computers that are taking over so many tasks on which men once used their own heads, and that are making our society ever more mechanized and automated. English teachers likewise may not welcome the news that within a few years computers will be available for the classroom, or even that they are already being used to read and grade student themes; teachers have a natural prejudice in favor of the live teacher, despite his being less patient and more fallible than machines. At the seminar no enthusiasm was expressed over Grommon's report of a midwestern college where 4000 students are being taught largely by electronic devices, films, and materials manufactured by the faculty, with drills and exercises dispensed through apparatus always on call. Some of us may not simply rejoice either over the growing wealth of "audiovisual aids," which may swell the rage for gimmicks, the tendency to subordinate the written word to pictures or "audile-tactile perception."

Still, the profession obviously does welcome some of the aids provided by modern technology. Nobody questioned the boon of films, recordings, and tapes—of plays classical and modern, poets reading their own works, professionals reading selections from *Beowulf*, Chaucer, and Shakespeare as he sounded in his own day. These may help students to listen better too. The seminar itself demanded more technological aids for English teachers—such facilities as projectors, tape recorders, sound recording booths, and duplicating equipment. Grommon pointed out other developments that the profession might welcome. Some millions of students unable to attend college are taking courses on television. Whole libraries may now be stored on microfilm or magnetic tape, and any work be made available by automatic printing or projection on a screen for schools with necessarily small libraries; we are told that there will be centers for such purposes, if under the forbidding name of "computer-controlled information and retrieval systems." Computers themselves are not simply forbidding. Already used to schedule students in classes, they may relieve the teacher of other routine chores. Machines are helping in the teaching of spelling, grammar, and reading, where they have the advantage of enabling each student to work at his own pace—a particular advantage for the handicapped children the seminar was so solicitous about. And the enthusiasts working on such projects keep assuring us, if perhaps too insistently, that the computers and teaching machines will never displace the live teacher, but merely liberate him from drills and routines, enable him to devote himself entirely to the rewarding kind of teaching that machines can never do. I would stress that they present only questions to which the answer is right or wrong, and are incapable of dealing with the tentative, the ambiguous, or the controversial.

At the seminar the whole issue of technological developments in the teaching of English was focused by a talk given by Susan Markle. A psychologist, she announced that the real technological innovation had been overlooked: it was not all the new gadgets and devices, but the introduction of psychology. She is in charge of a project for programing courses, in a "bureau of instructional resources." A professor's lectures are taped and presented to large numbers of students; small groups then meet with tutors for discussion. Psychologists advise the professor on the preparation of his lectures, in particular by testing their effectiveness, for instance checking with the students to find out whether he is going over their heads. Their analysis of the programs will in time assure carefully tested materials. Meanwhile Dr. Markle assured the seminar that the object of the programing was not to supplant teachers, only to improve their teaching by basing it on research evidence, and thereby to assure more justice to their students. While granting that there was some danger of a craze for teaching machines, she emphasized that what educational psychologists are selling is primarily tested materials. She added that the many professors who are hostile had better get into the education industry if they want to have more say about the programs.

It did not help her cause, however, when she remarked breezily at the outset that her office already had eighteen cans of videotaped professor, or "teaching behavior." Although polite, her audience obviously did not relish the idea of being put into cans. Those who spoke up in the discussion indicated some mistrust of the psychologists. Dr. Markle admitted that at first her fellows had been mostly crude behaviorists who knew little about either students or the subject being programed and grossly underestimated the ability of students, but she declared that now they are better informed, able as experienced analysts to give teachers the help they need. My impression is that the seminar shared my doubts about the wisdom of educational psychologists, in part because of their technical jargon. But the critical question centered on the "testing" of the materials of the programs. What was tested? Was it attitudes, personal development, sensitivity to values, stimulus to creativity? Or was it not merely knowledge and proficiency? The answer was that it was chiefly the latter, but with some effort to check up on such objectives as pleasure in reading and desire to read more. I assume that systematic programing will naturally tend to emphasize what can be most readily and surely tested, and that its success will depend primarily on the quality of the teachers who are canned, perhaps now and then their insistence on their own judgment in defiance of their mentors.[3]

------

[3] I cannot forbear from mentioning, with permission, a privately circulated comment on programing by John Sinclair, a British linguist. He devised exercises in "programed meditation" that included the following:
Frame 1. Look at your navel. What reactions do you have?
    a) It disgusts me.—4
    b) I can't see it.—5

Dr. Markle gave the soundest answer to the critical question before it was asked. At the conclusion of her talk she said that the problem in programing was to set up clear criteria. Add that the criteria in English should be not only clear but sound, humane, and civilized, and this is a philosophical problem. It was implicit in all the discussions of the seminar. As I see it, it cannot be settled by more research evidence; at best this will help in decisions about means rather than ends. There is no scientific or any other way of proving that the ends in the teaching of English should be civil, not merely practical—the capacity for a fuller, richer life, not merely the ability to make a better living. For the English teacher the basic problem raised by modern technology is that it has obscured or confused the all-important question of ends by its triumphant concentration on efficient means. Its by-products, the mass media, have tended to impoverish the ends by the thin fare they offer, reduce them to mere escape from boredom, while advertisers sell the values of conformity to a slavish materialism. Then it may be added that modern technology has also produced an unprecedented wealth of readily available cultural goods—paperbacks, records, reproductions of paintings, photographs, reputable films and television programs, and so forth. And given the flood of students and the scarcity of teachers, even the canned lectures may help in presenting expository material in introductory courses. Those who prefer to put themselves in books rather than cans may do so more readily than they could in the past.

Frame 3. Think very carefully about it. What does it make you think of?
    a) My navel.—2
    b) Nothing at all.—3
    c) Anything else.—2

Frame 4. Your navel is not disgusting. It is your viewpoint that makes it seem so. Say once "My navel is beautiful." What do you think of it now?
    a) It disgusts me.—4
    b) I can't see it.—5

CHAPTER NINE

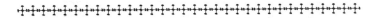

EXAMINATIONS
AND TEACHERS

In its concluding sessions the seminar considered some professional problems and projects, as of research, in which the general public could not be expected to take a lively interest. Among them, however, were still matters that I think should be of some interest to readers who have got this far. I begin with one that all readers have sweated over in their day—examinations. They may welcome the news that the seminar expressed strong feelings over these ordeals.

The British have especially strong feelings about their "external" examinations that set national standards. In a paper deploring their effects on the teaching of English, George Allen reviewed the General Certificate of Education examinations at the ordinary or "O" level (taken at about the age of sixteen) and the advanced or "A" level (about eighteen). One or both of these are taken by all students hoping to enter a university or college of education, and a very high percentage fail—on the "O" level nearly half. The latter in particular have been stereotyped examinations that could be anticipated; so teachers drilled and students crammed for them. They are worse because they are split into language and literature examinations, taken separately. This unnatural division of English is accentuated on the "A" level, where the examination is on literature alone; the traditional schools stop teaching language at the age of sixteen (just when the British said it might be safe to teach it "explicitly"). Allen was pleased to report some improvements in these examinations in recent years, but he emphasized how much there is to be said against them:

> The dichotomy of "Lang." and "Lit." running like the Berlin wall clean across what should be a single subject, the lack of an oral test, the traditional papers each duller than the last, the dress rehearsals at school (on which much may hang) and indeed many of the school's own internal examinations over a long period (since their pattern tends to follow the external lead), the cram textbooks, the general sense of strain, the effort to write an acceptable piece of prose about nothing in particular or to memorize and apply traditional grammatical terms which grammarians have long since discarded or to guess what sort of paper it will be in literature, the second-hand opinion—all these may not so much influence the teaching as make a bid to take over the entire English syllabus.

America has had no such required external examinations, but it has been developing something comparable in the College Entrance Board Examinations that are taken by students all over the country, and must be on the minds of many parents too. Alan Purves of the Educational Testing Service gave a talk on these, which in English include verbal aptitude, composition, and literature. Although himself engaged in the examination industry (now a flourishing business), Purves thinks the College Boards have had some unfortunate effects. Many high schools are drilling students in the prescribed aptitudes, cramming them with vocabulary. A dubious examination in composition allots forty minutes to questions on syntax and style, only twenty minutes for an essay on banal topics chosen so as not to require thought. (Readers of the exam are asked to grade the writer only on his "promise.") Some eastern universities put much stock in the College Boards, as do some social-climbing colleges; except for sons of prominent alumni and maybe star athletes, students have little chance of being accepted unless they get a high rating in them. And now the faith in this mode of behavioral science has inspired a proposal that national assessment examinations be given on four age levels, and repeated every five years, in order to measure something like the gross national educational product. Presumably these would give educational psychologists a field day.

Purves and other Americans emphasized, however, that such external examinations remain essentially different from the British ones. On its aptitude tests the College Entrance Examination Board takes great pains not to test literary or linguistic knowledge, so as not to influence the curriculum of the schools.[1] The great majority of the universities and

---

[1] I recall a good sample question on literature that I read years ago, designed to test a student's ability to understand poetry. He was asked to suggest an appropriate title for stanzas from an unidentified poem by Emily Dickinson:

> These are the days when Birds come back—
> A very few—a bird or two—
> To take a backward look.

> These are the days when skies resume
> The old—old sophistries of June—
> A blue and gold mistake.

The poem had been entitled "Indian Summer." But I felt free to give an A to a boy who suggested "Alumni Reunion."

(Reprinted by permission of the publishers and the Trustees of Am-

colleges neither require these examinations nor reject students on the basis of them, but use them chiefly as guides in placement and prediction; they have admissions officers who consider as well a student's high school record and other evidence of his qualifications. Hence his whole future does not depend, as it too often does in England, on how he performs on a single examination. If a mediocre showing excludes him from a few select universities and colleges, there remain many reputable ones that will accept him. Under these circumstances, the College Boards can have considerable value. The verbal aptitude test has proved more dependable than any other in predicting a student's capacity for college work. Both schools and students have benefited most clearly from the three-hour advanced placement examination, which enables colleges to exempt many students from the requirement of Freshman English.

Even so some British representatives at once expressed shock over Alan Purves's report. They had thought that America was in this respect an Eden, untouched by the curse of external examinations. Now they called upon the seminar to issue the most emphatic statement condemning all such examinations; they thought no issue was more vital, no recommendation more urgently needed. Hence the two delegations again diverged. While Americans sympathized with the feeling of the British, some pointed out that the situation in this country is quite different and does not call for such a manifesto. The problem here is not rigid, narrow standards but extremely uneven, confused ones, and the need of bringing many schools up to higher standards, as the College Boards are helping to do. Purves commented on the notorious unreliability of the credit system in American schools, even apart from the glaring regional differences;

herst College from Thomas H. Johnson, Editor, *The Poems of Emily Dickinson,* Cambridge, Mass.: The Belknap Press of Harvard University Press. Copyright, 1951, 1955, by the President and Fellows of Harvard College.)

teachers inflate grades by considering not only attainment but industry, deportment, "personality," even dress—not to mention fear of community pressures against strict grading. In any case, there is no one constituted authority in America to address a ringing denunciation to. The high schools, like the universities, are free to set their own examination procedures. Such bodies as the U.S. Office of Education, the Modern Language Association, and the National Council of Teachers of English can only offer advice to schools and colleges, never lay down the law to them. There would be a national uproar if the Office of Education ever claimed any such authority. The proposal of national assessment examinations is meeting strong opposition even though they would not affect the standing of students in the schools.

The upshot of the discussion was a compromise report drawn up jointly by an American and an Englishman, which was endorsed by Alan Purves. It declared that "examinations should conform to all that teachers of a subject are attempting to teach," as they do in neither country at present. "The English teacher works in a social and educational setting which has created and perpetuated examinations, tests, procedures for grading and assessment of every kind which disregard any reasonable conception of the aims of English and indeed promote rival values and kinds of work; the influence upon school curricula of these examinations and tests is increasing, and is aggravated by the effects of 'grouping' or 'streaming' about which the seminar has already expressed its concern." The statement concluded with a recommendation that a systematic "review of examinations and grading of all kinds should be undertaken forthwith," considering such questions as the purposes to which they lend themselves, whether they serve these purposes efficiently, and which of the purposes may impede the proper teaching of English. The professional organizations that sponsored the seminar were requested to sponsor such a review.

Most of the participants—including Americans—wanted a more strongly worded statement than this; so a later version stated more emphatically the evils of the present system. No one, I suppose, would deny that a great deal of mechanical examining goes on in both countries, grading students by confused or dubious criteria, seldom by such qualities as imagination, sensitivity, and taste. Few parents appear to realize, however, the effects these procedures have on the curriculum and methods of teaching. Most schools continue preparing students for such mechanical examinations, ignoring effects that are most deplorable in English, since other major subjects have a more definite, essential body of knowledge on which students may reasonably be tested. But because the problem is more serious than the general public realizes, I would add that it is also more difficult than the seminar implied, and that there is reason to doubt that the most systematic review will come out with a solution.

In their understandable indignation, the British could verge on futility at times because they appeared to resent the very idea of formal examinations. The enemy, they said, is the System, the Machine; but what they were taking on was modern society as a whole. This is a competitive society that imposes something like tests in many activities. Above all, it is a highly organized society. If the "organizational revolution" that came with modern technology has led to excessive bigness—bureaucracy in government, corporations, labor unions, universities, and all through the society—it is impossible in our kind of society to avoid a vast deal of organization and the uniform procedures it requires. Students liberated from the stupidities or injustices of external examinations will still have to take civil service, professional, or other examinations. Somehow uniform, impersonal standards must be maintained, for the sake of justice as well as efficiency. And nowhere is the need of such standards plainer than in mass education, to the ideal of which the seminar was wholly committed.

Glyn Lewis again kept pressing a reasonable question on his compatriots. We have goals, some of which can be evaluated; so the question is how best to go about it. Or did we mean that our subject cannot be evaluated or graded? An American added that aptitude tests would seem reasonable, and if the seminar was so shocked by the College Entrance Boards, we might as well throw up our hands. Finally George Allen forced the actual issue: What are the alternatives to formal examinations? The British answer appeared to be to leave everything to the individual schools or teachers; but this is hardly a clear or ideal solution. One who agrees that examinations should test "all that teachers of a subject are attempting to teach" must reckon with the fact that there are all kinds of teachers, with different ideas about what and how they should teach. Should all, good and bad, be permitted to examine by their own standards?

Since the seminar obviously wanted to maintain standards, the specific question is whether there is any better way to do so than external examinations. As it is, Alan Purves reminded the British of the reputed differences in standards between their grammar and comprehensive schools—a matter that was slighted in the condemnation of grouping. A few years ago many English and Welsh universities accordingly imposed still another external examination, called "Use of English"; an American could forgive them, since they were alarmed by how poorly many of their students wrote. Or in America the issue might be forced by the Regents examinations set up in New York State. These hold all high schools up to uniform standards in all subjects, but I assume restrict the freedom of teachers in choice of curriculum. Other states permit both more local freedom and local failure by not imposing such external examinations. Which is the better policy? The seminar did not tackle this question.

As one who does not know the answer, I point to another difficulty in the broader problem of grading. There is now some tendency to play down grades so as to cut the costs of excessive competitiveness, the humiliation of slow youngsters. This seems to me a humane policy, despite my suspicion that most American youngsters do not feel humiliated by poor grades in English. The ideal, I presume, might be simply to rate work as satisfactory or unsatisfactory. Certainly I would feel happier so as a teacher: I must hope my life will never depend on my ability to define or defend the difference between B— and C+—a distinction I have had to make hundreds of times, and one that may make a considerable difference to students majoring in the subject. But the difficulty remains that both universities and employers want more precise ratings. Given the many millions of students bent on moving up or out into the professional world, the rating of "satisfactory" is not enough. It will not satisfy either most of the better students—or their parents. Granted that our society is too fond of tests and grades, they can hardly be dispensed with. And again the most serious complaint about American high schools in this respect is that most teachers give too high grades.

Another reason why examining and grading are sure to go on is that most teachers want them. The British complained that when their Minister of Education opposed the introduction of a new external examination, he had little support from teachers associations. It was said that parents demanded them, but it might have been added that teachers too felt happier with them. As George Allen wrote, they "cling to the examination syllabus because it provides an incentive which would never on any other terms attach to the dreary exercises which have traditionally provided the easiest kind of English teaching." So we are brought to another problem of public concern that cropped up in every discussion, and that at the end the seminar did meet head-on—the quality of the teacher.

In a long report on the education of English teachers, drafted from suggestions that came in from many participants, it was remarked that teachers were mostly "average educated people," no better than their education. In general they are not drawn from the ranks of the best students, nor are departments of education and teachers colleges distinguished as centers of intellectual ferment or higher learning. Many teachers regard their work as a vocation rather than a profession. Especially in America many are married women teaching in order to supplement the family income, and many others are single women who will quit teaching when they get married. The seminar often used the bad word for *average—mediocre.*

There was some feeling that this attitude was too patronizing. The report itself noted that most teachers evidently like to work with children; many are dedicated people, carrying on heroically in overcrowded classrooms with inadequate facilities; and few find teaching an easy vocation. Because of the legitimate complaints about the quality of English teaching, I would first put in a few more words in their behalf. Let us consider the range of their duties in America. One type is the country school teacher described by E. B. White: "She not only undertakes to instruct her charges in all the subjects of the first three grades, but she manages to function quietly and effectively as a guardian of their health, their clothes, their habits, their mothers, and their snowball engagements." A more common type is the English teacher in the big city school, who on the average has five classes a day, thirty students in each. Her work week is longer because she has many compositions to read, while on the side she is usually expected to help out with such extracurricular activities as school magazines, dramatics, and debates. It is no wonder if she is not an avid reader of literature or a close reader of compositions, and in class does no more than go through the prescribed motions.

The most enthusiastic young teachers are likely to be

the unhappiest just because they have to go through motions prescribed by the educational bureaucracy. Like as not the state or local board dictates the curriculum, with outmoded textbooks to match; they may be bombarded by directives from superintendents, demanding procedures unsuited to either their eager interests or the problems they face in the classroom; in the big cities they may have to deal with much too large classes of unruly youngsters, poor and not at all eager. It is no wonder either that many of these teachers quit after a year or so, swelling the large turnover. In a panel discussion John Marcatante gave a vivid idea of what he was up against in a junior high school attended by many "disadvantaged" students, even though it was a new, relatively well-equipped school. He was able largely to ignore the state and city syllabi, which he found unintelligible, but he had to carry on with the usual understaffed department, in the face of a yearly turnover of fifty to sixty percent. He told of the wondrous change in a classroom that was rearranged especially for English, with provision for special groups and activities; the students were happy just to come into the room. But the next year the old furniture had to be moved back because of overcrowding. English is always likely to be the last subject to be favored by the authorities.

Marcatante also told, however, of ill-prepared teachers who demanded structure or program because they had only fuzzy ideas about what they were supposed to teach. The fact remains that half the English teachers in high school have not majored in the subject but have had only the required number of courses in education—all about methods in general. A great many do not feel fully committed to English teaching as a profession. It appears that the poorly prepared ones are the least likely to go on studying their subject, the most likely to be content with the conventional routines or easy solutions to complex problems. Many of those who did major in English feel no such need of keeping up with the subject as science teachers ordinarily do; they think they have already learned all they need to know. Or perhaps the fairest statement is another that was often made during the seminar, that English teachers commonly feel insecure. They are unsure of their judgment of literature and student writing, therefore dependent on the authority of their textbooks and manuals, which usually oblige by being too dogmatic. They feel most sure when correcting errors in exercises and compositions, pronouncing the correct judgments in literature, and maintaining the sanctities of "culture." They are unable to resist the social pressures against independence in judgment, the demands for "good English" and "wholesome" literature.

Their conventional attitudes might be of some concern to the general reader because they reflect the attitude of the public to teachers. This is an ambiguous attitude, a mingling of respect and condescension. Teaching has been regarded as a kind of "calling," like missionary work, and has therefore been as poorly paid. In America, where education has long been a fetish and people get sentimental over the "little red schoolhouse," teachers used to be paid better than unskilled laborers but not so well as skilled ones. Since the war they have been considerably better paid, but never so well as other professions—except the ministry. The popular notion is that teaching is a relatively easy job, with long vacations, and calls for only modest abilities. It is a kind of haven for women not interested in a career, and for men lacking the ambition and ability to make good in business. University professors too have typically looked down on school teachers, assuming that the really bright students would naturally go into college teaching.

The seminar report accordingly emphasized that teaching has become not only a major industry but today a major problem, of a radically new kind. As I write, America faces a critical shortage of teachers, which made headlines when the schools opened in the fall of 1966. With the increasing hordes of students, the problem of recruiting enough teachers is due to become still more urgent. The seminar magnified the problem by stressing the need of "able, imaginative, well-educated teachers with deep professional commitment." The qualifications it set up called for not at all modest abilities. The English teacher should know children and young people, of course, as well as something about educational theory and practice; he should know a good deal about both language and literature, have good taste and judgment in both; he should have some acquaintance with "culture and environment studies"; and other reports suggested that he should be able to teach speaking, creative dramatics, creative writing, and the mass media. Although I assume that no one really expected teachers to master all these subjects, the good English teacher as defined by the report is a person of quite exceptional abilities—broader interests and finer, more diverse skills than are required of teachers of other major subjects, in which reformers can dream of "teacher-proof" materials.

The seminar made as heavy, possibly exorbitant demands in its recommendations for in-service training and the continuing education of English teachers. They should try to go on with their study of language and literature, keep abreast of new developments and experiments in English and related fields, reevaluate their work in the classroom in the light of such knowledge and discussion with their colleagues, and develop some semispecialty, such as theater or film study. Someone observed that the report seemed unreasonable when it asked overworked teachers to participate actively in local associations, regional conferences, and national organizations (a requirement that made me shudder, since I do not share the national faith in conventions and committees). But it was generally agreed that schools—or in effect society—should do much more to encourage and assist the continuing education of teachers. Although America is making more provision for it than Britain does through extension courses, summer institutes, workshops, and the like, and some schools even grant teachers sabbatical leaves, most do not subsidize study beyond the line of daily duty.

Needless to add, the vision of the seminar will not be realized in the near future, if ever. Once more, however, something can be said for utopian visions, ideal objectives that may both inspire and guide effort. For the short run, these recommendations might at least help parents to size up how well English is being taught in the local schools, and induce them to support efforts to improve teaching conditions. For the long run, given the popular talk about the "Great Society," they might help to persuade Americans of one elementary requirement of such a society—that its people be able to read, write, and talk intelligently. Meanwhile the authors of another ambitious proposal—a major experiment to be carried on simultaneously in selected school districts in Canada, the United States, and England—pointed to the immediate moral of these recommendations for an affluent society. "It may well be," they concluded, a little wistfully, "that before long, if we want the right things, we shall get them." If so, it will require both professional zeal and public support. We are brought to the issues of responsibility.

CHAPTER TEN

THE ISSUES
OF RESPONSIBILITY

At the end, the Anglo-American Seminar appeared by and large to take a more cheerful view of the state of English than it had at the outset. No dismay was expressed over the statement in one report that "thinking about aims and methods in English is still very fluid," and that "if anything, our discussions will have the immediate effect of making current views more fluid, not less"—which was to say that the seminar left English in a state of confusion. The chief reason for the apparent contentment was that it had nevertheless reached more agreement than had been expected and issued a number of positive recommendations. The agreement included approval of much that is being done in both countries, as positive efforts to improve the teaching of English. Fluidity is after all a healthier state than stagnation. To begin my conclusion, I record the agreeable impression that English is on the whole in a better state today than it has ever been before, or at least than it was in my own youth. Certainly the students now entering American state universities are in general better prepared than were many I taught before World War II.

The contentment of the seminar was not complacence, however, nor was it bolstered by optimism over the prospects of its recommendations being acted on promptly and decisively. The report on fluidity (drawn up by an Englishman, a Canadian, and an American) mentioned that another reason why no generally acceptable solution for English is in sight is "external factors." The specter of these factors, which had haunted every discussion, was exorcised by none of the recommendations. Its presence gave a utopian air to quite reasonable proposals, such as the "workshop" approach that might realize the ideal of the democratic classroom. The specter was again the System—and behind it Society. My conclusion will also be somewhat lame, hobbled by questions.

Now, like all professions teaching has its traditional responsibilities to the public. Teachers in public schools are kept more aware of them than are most other professionals because they are literally public servants, entrusted with care of the youth, and do not set their own fees. The only question is the nature of their responsibilities—precisely what they owe to the youth, and also to their parents or to "society," whose interests are not necessarily identical. The recommendations of the seminar assumed that English teachers still have all their traditional duties, but that they have also to face some new challenges because of the profound changes that have come over society. One is of course the advent of mass education beyond the primary schools, which is enabling many more young people to get a higher education, but raising more question about how "high" it is or ought to be. Another change just as obvious, but with revolutionary implications that are not so generally realized, is the phenomenal growth and spread of modern technology, an efficient rationale that involves some sacrifice of simple reasonableness. The seminar did not dwell, however, on the topic that in recent years has made education front-page news—the national interest.

Since this interest has been defined in an atmosphere of cold war and crisis, we might get some perspective by returning to the famous report *Cardinal Principles of Secondary Education,* published in the relatively simple old days (1918) when crisis was not yet the normal state. (Few people paid heed to the remark of H. G. Wells that from then on history was a race between education and catastrophe.) The commission that issued the report defined the "main objectives" of the high schools quite placidly. They were: (1) health; (2) command of fundamental processes (reading, writing, computation, expression); (3) worthy home membership; (4) vocation; (5) citizenship; (6) worthy use of leisure; (7) ethical character. English teachers were no doubt expected to contribute directly to all of these objectives except health and perhaps vocation. The commission did not specify the "qualities that make the individual a worthy member of a family," but it was explicit enough about citizenship and "loyalty to ideals of civic righteousness," in the interest of American democracy. Most important was ethical character:

> Stated in terms of national service, the aim of the secondary school should be to equip our pupils as fully as possible with the habits, insights, and ideals that will enable them to make America more true to its best traditions and hopes. To strengthen what is most admirable in the American character and to add to it should be the goal toward which all the activities are pointed.

On this goal the commission permitted itself an unabashed peroration:

To consider moral values in education is to fix attention upon what should be the paramount aim. A schooling that imparts knowledge or develops skill or cultivates tests or intellectual aptitudes fails of its supreme object if it leaves its beneficiaries no better morally. In all their relationships present and future, that is, as schoolmates, as friends, as members of a family, as workers in their special vocations, as Americans, as world citizens, the greatest need of our boys and girls is character, the habitual disposition to choose those modes of behavior that most do honor to human dignity. Not simply to learn to tell the truth or to respect property rights, but to realize in ever more vital ways that the worth of life consists in the endeavor to live out in every sphere of conduct the noblest of which one is capable—this it is which gives education its highest meaning.

Quaint as this old-fashioned language may sound today, it should first be noted that Americans are still fond of such oratory. They are ostensibly dedicated to the same mission they were in 1918, making the world safe for democracy; Congress and the press resound with celebrations of the moral, spiritual values that distinguish American democracy from godless communism; and at commencement exercises high school graduates can count on hearing much about how character is what matters most. The difference today is that the national interest is defined in much more insistently practical terms. The billions that the government is spending on education and research are going chiefly to science and technology, primarily for the sake of the cold war; Congress would never appropriate such sums to support research for its educational value or for the disinterested pursuit of truth. Similarly the main argument for the little support English is beginning to get is the practical importance of "communication skills." As for character, it too is conceived in practical terms, somewhat short of the "highest meaning" of education. Even in commencement oratory I suppose

174

few speakers today would say that the schools are or should be trying to form "noble" characters. The emphasis now is on well-adjusted ones—the kind of character that will help students to get along better in both business and social life. "Personality" serves the same purpose. One could wish for more stress on moral responsibility, as in the use of language.

Nevertheless the authors of *Cardinal Principles* were essentially committed to values that still dominate American education. The high school curriculum was not actually planned in high moral terms, of course, nor could it be. (Let us remember that America was shortly to enter the "normalcy" of the Harding era—about the most corrupt, ignoble era in the nation's history.) When the commission got down to cases, it was concerned about the immediate, practical values of education—preparing students for work, many for vocations. Otherwise it was concerned with the needs of society, such as "habits of cordial cooperation," "a clear conception of right relations" between workers and employers, and "a respect for property rights." It showed scant interest in any but the vocational needs of the individual. While it coupled the goal of "worthy use of leisure" with such ideas as "the potential, and perchance unique, worth of the individual," it made only perfunctory mention of ideals of self-expression and self-realization. Its main objective was the development not of individuality but of "those common ideas, common ideals, and common modes of thought, feeling, and action, whereby America, through a rich, unified, common life, may render her truest service to a world seeking for democracy among men and nations." If in teaching literature the high schools have had some idea of the worthy use of leisure, their curriculum has been designed primarily to serve practical needs and promote common modes of thought and feeling. A contemporary book on the teaching of English by Charles Swain Thomas expressed the spirit of the commission: "The literary selection must breathe the right ethical and social message . . . . Our most important

175

task is the building of character, and our most effective agency is the literary selection."

In this perspective the recommendations of the Anglo-American Seminar may again look more radical—an almost complete reversal of emphasis. While providing for the basic skills that all students need for their practical purposes, it subordinated these to human values. Its objective was not merely proficiency but pleasure in the uses of language and literature, and these uses as a means to learning how to live, exploring as well as communicating experience, illuminating, deepening, and enriching it. Similarly its stress was on personal experience, the development of children as individuals, with provision for their different personal needs and potentialities. It took seriously the ideal of not only a "worthy" but a humanly satisfying use of leisure. In effect, it was most interested in saving people, not just "society." Feeling typically ran highest against policies and procedures, such as conventional examinations, that obscure or thwart these humane objectives. The objectives were profoundly moral, but did not breathe the conventional "message."

As I have indicated from time to time, the revulsion against the traditional method of teaching English tended to minimize the legitimate claims of society. The British, who on every issue were most active and vocal in championing the interests of children, could be charged with slighting their practical needs as members of society. I think John Dewey, now much maligned in America, took a more comprehensive, balanced view of education, with a clearer eye to both practical and intellectual interests, and to individuality as something that can be fully developed only in and through community. But once more I repeat my belief that the British were saying what most needs to be said in our technocratic society. They were defending the all-important human values that are being neglected in the interests of economy and efficiency, when not sacrificed to both military and commercial interests. The preservation of these values is by no means the responsibility of English teachers alone; but the gist of the seminar's recommendations is again that the study of language and literature can and should contribute more directly than any other major subject to the realization of both our common humanity and our personal identity.

So we are led to the claims of English on the national interest, which was unmentioned in the final recommendations. One may always bring in those communication skills and repeat that they are especially important in a democracy, since it depends more than other societies on clear, informed, intelligent communication. The seminar did commit itself to furthering the interests of democracy, not by preaching it or indoctrinating students, but by introducing more of it into the classroom. Otherwise I should say that English has no immediate claims in terms of the national emergency; its present state does not to my mind constitute a "crisis" or call for a crash program, which at best would help little anyway. Its claims are rather for the long run, or what academics have always claimed for it. They are stronger today primarily for the very reasons why English has been slighted: an extraordinary technology that rewards the immense investment in it with spectacular achievements, and as literally extraordinary an affluence that makes people busier than ever in acquiring and consuming material goods. The objectives held up by the seminar make more sense now that this wondrous technology and unprecedented affluence have aroused a national aspiration to become a "Great Society."

These developments have also obscured the elementary question: What makes a people or society "great"? The criterion cannot be technological efficiency or material wealth and power, of course, since these are only means to some end; by such popular criteria we are already by far the greatest society in all history. The criterion or the end must be some conception of the good life. On just what

177

conception we shall never agree, any more than writers and thinkers over the centuries have ever been able to agree; but almost all have agreed that it must be defined in terms of strictly human values—moral, cultural, spiritual. In other words, we are asking the old questions of our brave new world: What kind of people in it? What kind of life do they lead? What are they living for? Again there are many different answers, no means of agreement; but thoughtful people can agree that these are the kind of questions that must be asked of a people aspiring to greatness. The seminar implicitly declared among other things that English properly taught should awaken students to such questions, make them more aware of the diverse possibilities of life, help them choose for themselves in accordance with their own interests and needs—not to adopt unthinkingly the "common modes of thought, feeling, and action," which today so commonly end in feelings of the aimlessness and hollowness of the affluent life, or in sheer boredom. Given the ever shorter work week made possible by modern technology, no educational aim is more practical than that stated by Aristotle— the wise use of leisure.

Such considerations have become much more important in the universities, for reasons the seminar did not go into. Daniel Bell has pointed out that since 1940 the United States government has increased by about seventy times its expenditures for "research and development" in the universities.[1] With the increasing millions of students, these billions of dollars are making the universities over into central institutions, far more influential than ever before, which bid fair to become the primary institutions of a technocratic society. The "education industry" is now a big business, run

---

[1] James Conant illustrated the change by a story of a representative of the American Chemical Society who called on the War Department, when the United States entered World War I, to offer the government the services of chemists. He was thanked but told that the offer was unnecessary: the War Department already had a chemist.

by an ever bigger administrative bureaucracy. The administrators are pleased to talk of the growing "knowledge industry." Clark Kerr, former president of the "multiversity" of California, writes characteristically that "the production, distribution, and consumption" of knowledge now accounts for "29 percent of the gross national product," and "is growing at about twice the rate of the economy." But those concerned with liberal education, or the cultivation of human values, cannot simply rejoice in this phenomenal growth. The great bulk of the federal money continues to go into research in the sciences and the development of technology. The emphasis is on "knowledge," not powers of thought, broad comprehension, or philosophy, still less on enlargement of the imagination; the "knowledge explosion" makes it ever harder to achieve a comprehensive view of any major subject. Since knowledge is got by research, the drive is to specialize earlier and more intensively. Liberal education represents a small department of the multiversity that produces and distributes something most students want to put behind them in a year or two so as to settle down to their specialty, the serious business of education. I assume that its "consumption" represents a negligible fraction of the gross national product.

English departments might accordingly feel a particular responsibility to carry on a traditional enterprise of liberal education, which is more important in universities geared to a technocratic society—the enterprise, in Daniel Bell's words, of liberating students by making them "aware of the forces that impel them from within and constrict them from without." Although the seminar referred to this problem only by implication, its recommendations for the teaching of English in the schools could be spelled out in these terms. For the rest it requested English departments in the universities to do more to recruit and prepare school teachers— a responsibility that hitherto they have not assumed.

Beyond the "service" course in freshman composition,

their main business has been the teaching of literature and the breeding of Ph.D.'s. Only a handful of their students take creative writing, another handful linguistics. The apparent objective of many if not most literature courses has been to turn out literary scholars or literary critics, though few students will ever become either; the departments have shown less interest in what might seem to be their most reasonable, important objective—to turn out good "common readers." As for the doctors of philosophy, the degree has become a necessity for young men who hope to get a position in the universities or better colleges. It has little or nothing to do with "philosophy," of course, and often little more with the appreciation of literature; the doctoral dissertation is supposed to be a contribution to learning and so has typically been centered on factual research. Except for the value of specialized knowledge, this kind of graduate work has not been designed to prepare students for teaching, least of all the freshman composition that most of the beginners have to teach. Promotion depends more on research and publication than good teaching anyhow. Now the extraordinary growth of the universities has intensified the production of the higher learning in English to provide the needed instructors. It has also created a distraction by increased work on committees; with the growth of huge departments, committees have multiplied. So far, in short, there is some question how well the English departments have been serving either the national interest or the cause of liberal education.

Yet there has been a growing resistance to most of these tendencies. More attention is being paid to literary values, both in teaching and in graduate study. More is being paid as well to the broad connections of literature with other studies, such as psychology, sociology, and anthropology; at the seminar this appeared in the papers on myth, for example. But most pertinent here is the growing interest in teaching. Although American college teachers of English

180

have long complained about how poorly prepared many of their students were, they neglected to inform high school teachers just what they wanted taught, not to say how. Usually they had no clear idea what these teachers could and should do (as I for one certainly had not), only an impatient desire that somehow all students entering college should be well read and able to write. Today most are still engrossed in their own specialties, but some have come to feel that only by a responsible interest in better teaching can the profession claim the national support it wants. Their interest has led to the unprecedented collaboration between university and school teachers, as in the Curriculum Study Centers, regional conferences, and summer institutes that have sprouted all over the land. The seminar naturally welcomed this change, especially because the universities are in any event bound to have an increasing influence on the high schools.

A lone note of dissent from the general agreement was voiced by Barbara Strang, a British linguist. Reminding the seminar that universities have traditionally been devoted to intellectual pursuits as ends in themselves—a role in which society has been willing to support them—she thought it alarming that English departments should be asked to abandon their distinctive role and "muck in with the rest of the educational cycle," go into the vocational business. She received no support, I assume because the seminar was not asking university departments to give up their traditional role—only to supplement it—and nobody wanted them to become mere service departments. But at this point the seminar skirted a possibly embarrassing question. If literary research is for the scholar a sufficient end in itself, one may doubt that much of the published research (not to mention all the doctoral dissertations) is a significant contribution to either knowledge or thought. Mrs. Strang could evade this issue because linguistic research has made more obvious contributions. Others implied some doubts by playing down the need of lit. hist. and lit. crit.

181

On the whole, however, the seminar appeared to remain under the spell of the word "research"—today more than ever a magic word in the universities. Thus from the beginning it was repeatedly pointed out that we do not really know the value of this or that study or practice, we need more evidence, and so we need more research. At the end various of the study groups included research projects in their recommendations, and summary papers listed others under "research and development," what attracts the big money for science and technology. An Englishman suggested the need of institutes of advanced educational studies. An American then pointed to another difference between the two countries: he remarked that hundreds of research projects are now going on, most of them trivial or useless, in schools or departments of education. Educational research has long been the vogue in this country. Now and then someone pointed to the reasons why it is rather different from research in the natural sciences—the many variables, the impossibility of completely controlled experiments, hence the impossibility of strictly verifying conclusions, etc. Another recognized complication was the "Hawthorne effect," the tendency of any new method or policy to get results just because it is new. Still, there was usually a call for more research whenever an issue was in doubt. The seminar did not come to grips with the question whether we could ever really find out as much as we would like to, or it was implied we needed to, and if not, what of it?

But I should now qualify my own freely expressed doubts that we can hope to learn a great deal by more research, or ever evaluate precisely experiments in the teaching of English. The widespread efforts to analyze and assess methods, materials, and aims are all to the good so long as they do not pretend to be "scientific." Some of the evidence has been plainly useful, as in supporting doubts of the value of intensive grammar drill—doubts that might otherwise be dismissed as mere prejudice or perverse whim. I. A. Richards taught teachers a good deal by his *Practical Criticism,* in which he demonstrated specifically how and why most university students read poetry poorly (though it was observed that his project would never have been awarded a research grant). Studies of child development have been especially helpful to teachers of the early grades. In general, it is a healthy sign that the profession has been looking outside itself, picking up suggestions for a suitable "philosophy" from social, cultural studies as well as from such philosophers as Whitehead and Dewey.

In particular one may welcome the many experiments going on in the schools, often without benefit of research. A new program may get obviously good results even though its success can never be measured exactly, and a quite different program might have got just as good results. Similarly valuable teaching practices may be recognized without methodological analysis or assessment, just as the Americans learned from the British teachers of creative writing and drama. Someone suggested that teaching was bound to become more of a science because teachers would have to know more about it, and if so one might have more misgivings about all the doubtful results of research that educationists are apt to put into the books prematurely. I assume that in any case it will remain an art too, which like other arts will embrace various good ways, and that the better teachers can be trusted to be judicious enough for the most part in departing from the traditional routines.

One may then have second thoughts about the problems raised by organization, another by-product of modern technology. Americans have long been notorious for their faith in organization, their habit of banding together to promote or prevent one thing or another, even before industrialism led to the giant organizations that dominate our society, making some people worry about all the anonymous little people in or under them. In the last century the profession established the Modern Language Association of America, which soon made literary research the main business of college English departments. British teachers, who have formed such associations only in the last few years, are most keenly aware of another kind of organization that is now troubling more Americans—the educational bureaucracy, and the increasingly elaborate administrative machinery that goes with it. Variously known as the Establishment, the System, or the Machine, this illustrates a wise remark of the authors of *Cardinal Principles*: "The objectives must determine the organization or else the organization will determine the objectives." University administrations typically assume that the faculty exists to serve them, not they the faculty.

Yet there is no getting away from bureaucracy, in education any more than in government or business. Like it or not, large-scale organization is plainly indispensable in a society as massive and complex as ours. And only by organization can teachers effectively combat the Establishment, alter its objectives, institute new policies and procedures. The innumerable conferences and committees that have been meeting all over America in recent years are another sign of life in the profession (if a kind of life I do not normally care to participate in). They are no less useful—perhaps in the main most useful—when they do not settle but merely define and discuss the problems of teaching. The professional organizations that sponsor them, now including the Modern Language Association of America, laid out an impressive agenda some years ago, listing as many as thirty-five basic problems. Having touched on all of them in this report, I am pleased to suppose that no other subject can boast of so many.

The seminar itself was of course a product of organization. It illustrated the good word for organization—cooperation. Its recommendations included more cooperation on an international scale. It proposed systematic exchange of information between the two countries, reports on the experiments being conducted in both, more exchange of teachers, and more visits to observe distinctive practices. Much fruitful cooperation could result from the seminar—always provided that governments, foundations, or school administrations lend the necessary financial support.

So we are brought back to the critical questions. To become effective, all the proposals of the seminar would require the cooperation of principals, superintendents, local school boards, state boards of education, schools of education—the assorted vested interests that do not normally welcome fundamental innovation. Most of the proposals would cost money. One hears of plenty of concern, in business as well as educational circles, over how poor a command of English most of our students have; but the concern usually stops short of pressure to appropriate more money. No English teacher can be expected to teach composition well, for example, when he has on an average 150 students; if he is to read their themes at all closely, give them any individual attention to speak of, he should have no more than about half so many students. The cost of recruiting the many more teachers needed would therefore run into the millions—still only a minute fraction of what is spent on arms, or the program for putting a man on the moon, but to legislators a lot of money, with no immediate prospects of what they ordinarily consider a pay-off. It took sputnik to get Congress interested in the quantity and quality of "scientific manpower." What will it take to persuade it that English is really fundamental?

Again, the responsibility for a better command of the language is not that of the profession alone. No teacher of English in high school can be expected to achieve the ideal objectives proposed by the seminar when he meets students but one period a day. Teachers in other subjects will have to cooperate if students are to learn to read, write, and speak better, and to assume that the ability to do so is not something exercised only in English classrooms to satisfy the

185

eccentrics in charge of them. So will the teachers of these teachers in the schools of education, and the superintendents of the schools. And so will parents.

Their responsibility is plainest in habits of reading, since the home is the most obvious place outside the school where such habits are formed. There is no natural order in the development of children's interests and tastes in literature; what they read depends chiefly on what is lying around them or what they happen to run into. Parents can help by not only reading to their children, as many used to, but having books around the home. They might also show more interest in the school library, now that a wealth of paperbacks is available. They might consider the list of 350 basic school paperbacks compiled twice a year by *School Paperback Journal*, comprising, it is said, at least ninety-five percent of those used in the high schools. Under "Guidance and Career" they will find such books as Dale Carnegie's *How to Win Friends and Influence People*, under "Literature and Leisure Reading" such titles as *Crash Club, Hot Rod*, and *Drag Strip*. These are designed to "motivate" teenagers to read, as well as to help them become well adjusted.

No doubt they reflect the interests and tastes of the society in which English teachers must help students to earn their living and take their place. Those teachers who are also interested in their development as human beings may therefore be troubled by the questions raised by Denys Thompson: "Can they conscientiously prepare their pupils to take the kind of place offered by the society they see? . . . Is it not likely that as people are better fitted to earn a living, the less likely they are to be developed human beings?" Now and then a note of disgust or near despair was sounded at the seminar, reminiscent of Jacques Barzun's announcement that the cause of liberal education is doomed in modern society. The prevailing mood, however, was neither despair nor the loathing of modern civilization expressed by the revered D. H. Lawrence. Those who periodi-

186

cally wondered whether our society really wanted the kind of developed persons the seminar wanted nevertheless endorsed its recommendations, all of which implied that improvement is possible, the cause of English is not hopeless. The doubters were themselves enthusiastic teachers, who have contributed to the ferment of recent years. They also contributed to my impression that English is healthier for the consciousness of thirty-five unsettled problems.

Even so I would end with questions. English as the seminar proposed it be taught would be more liberal and humane than English as it is taught in most schools, but it would also be riskier, possibly unsettling, certainly less likely to turn out students well adjusted to a highly commercialized society devoted to efficiency and affluence. Readers might ask themselves: Are they as taxpayers willing to foot the bills for better teaching of English? Do they as parents really want their children to become such developed individuals with minds of their own? Even lovers of literature? Even critics of "the common modes of thought, feeling, and action"?

PARTICIPANTS AT

THE DARTMOUTH SEMINAR

ABERCROMBIE, DAVID. Professor of Phonetics, University of Edinburgh. Author of *Studies in Phonetics and Linguistics*.

ADAMS, ANTHONY. Head of the English Department at Churchfields Comprehensive School, near Birmingham. Studied English at Cambridge University and has taught in grammar schools.

ALLEN, GEORGE. Professor of Education, University of Sussex. Formerly Her Majesty's Staff Inspector in the Department of Education and Science.

AUER, J. JEFFERY. Chairman and Professor, Department of Speech and Theatre, Indiana University. Former editor of *Speech Monographs* and past president of the Speech Association of America. Author of *Introduction to Research in Speech* and *Psychology of Communication*.

BARNES, DOUGLAS. Lecturer in Education, Leeds University. Taught in grammar schools and was until 1966 Head of the

English Department at Minchenden Grammar School in North London. Chairman of NATE 1967–1968.

BOOTH, WAYNE C. Dean of the College and George M. Pullman Professor of English, University of Chicago. Author of *The Rhetoric of Fiction* and member of the Commission on Literature, NCTE.

BRITTON, JAMES. Reader in Education and Head of the English Department, University of London Institute of Education. Director of a major research project concerned with children's writing.

CASSIDY, FREDERIC G. Professor of English, University of Wisconsin. Editor of *Dictionary of American Regional English* and author of *A Method for Collecting Dialect* and *Dictionary of Jamaican English*.

CHORNY, MERRON. Assistant Professor of English Education, University of Calgary. Editor of *The English Teacher* since 1961, coauthor of *The Professional Load of Secondary Teachers of English in Alberta*. Former principal at Grimshaw Public School and present chairman of the Standing Committee on the Formation of a Canadian Council of Teachers of English.

CHRISTENSON, BERNICE MARKS. Curriculum Supervisor—Elementary English, Los Angeles City Schools. Former elementary school teacher. Chairman, NCTE Committee to Develop Dialect Recordings for Elementary Schools, and coauthor of *Pre-Reading Materials, Kits A and B*.

DeMOTT, BENJAMIN. Professor of English and Chairman of English Department, Amherst College. Author of *Hells and Benefits, Essays* and *You Don't Say, Studies of Modern American Inhibitions;* member of the Carnegie Commission on Educational Television; on the Board of Editors, *College English*.

DIXON, JOHN. Senior Lecturer in English, Bretton Hall College of Education in Yorkshire. Former Head of the English Department at Walworth Comprehensive School in London. Author of *Criteria of Success in English* and *Growth through*

190

English, the report to the teaching profession of the Dartmouth Seminar.

DOUGLAS, WALLACE W. Professor of English and Education, Northwestern University, and Director of the Northwestern Curriculum Study Center in English. Member of the English Materials Center Committee, MLA; author of *The Character of Prose.*

EASTMAN, ARTHUR M. Professor of English, University of Michigan. Coeditor of *Masterpieces of the Drama* and *Shakespeare's Critics* and member of the NCTE Commission on the English Curriculum.

FISHER, JOHN HURT. Executive Secretary, MLA, and Professor of English, New York University. Author of *John Gower: Moral Philosopher and Friend of Chaucer;* editor of *The Medieval Literature of Western Europe: A Review of Research;* member of the National Commission to UNESCO and Chairman, Conference of Secretaries of the American Council of Learned Societies.

FORD, BORIS. Professor of Education and Dean of the School of Educational Studies, University of Sussex. He is editor of *Universities Quarterly* and edited *The Pelican Guide to English Literature.* Chairman of NATE 1963–1964.

FRANCIS, W. NELSON. Professor of Linguistics and English, Brown University. Author of *The Structure of American English, The History of English,* and *The English Language;* on Editorial Board, Conference on College Composition and Communication; Trustee, NCTE Research Foundation.

GROMMON, ALFRED H. Professor of Education and English, Stanford University. First Vice President of NCTE and general editor of *The Education of Teachers of English for American Schools and Colleges.*

HARDING, DENYS W. Professor of Psychology, University of London. Formerly one of the editors of *Scrutiny,* and in addition to work in psychology the author of a volume of literary criticism, *Experience into Words.*

HARDY, BARBARA. Professor of English Language and Literature, Royal Holloway College, University of London. Author

191

of *The Novels of George Eliot* and *Appropriate Form: an Essay on the Novel.*

HOLBROOK, DAVID. Poet, novelist, and author of several books on the teaching of English, including *English for Maturity* and *English for the Rejected.* Has taught in secondary modern schools and in adult education.

JENSEN, ARTHUR E. Professor of English, Dartmouth College, and former Dean of the College. Former Chairman, Committee on Examinations, CEEB; member of the Commission on English, CEEB; and local chairman for the Dartmouth Seminar.

JONES, ESMOR. Honorary Secretary of NATE. Formerly Head of the English Department at Ashmead County Secondary School, Reading, and now in educational publishing. Author of *English Examined.*

KITZHABER, ALBERT R. Professor of English, University of Oregon, and Director of the Oregon Curriculum Study Center in English. Former president of NCTE; author of *A Bibliography on Rhetoric in American Colleges, 1850–1900* and *Themes, Theories and Therapy: The Teaching of Writing in College.*

LACAMPAGNE, ROBERT J. Director of Special Projects and Achievement Awards, NCTE. Former high school teacher of English and drama. Editor of *High School Departments of English: Their Organization, Administration and Supervision* and coauthor of *Language Programs for the Disadvantaged.*

LAVIN, ALBERT L. Supervisor of English and Teacher of Advanced Placement English and Humanities, Tamalpais High School District, California. Coauthor of *Writing: Unit Lessons in Composition, Books I* and *III* and editor of *Readings for a New Rhetoric.*

LEWIS, E. GLYN. Her Majesty's Staff Inspector in the Welsh Office of the Department of Education and Science.

LOBAN, WALTER. Associate Professor of Education, University of California, Berkeley. His research studies, *The Language of Elementary School Children* and *Problems in Oral English,* present results of his twelve-year longitudinal study of children's language development. Coauthor of *The Teaching of Language and Literature.*

MACKAY, DAVID. Research Fellow in the Nuffield Programme in Linguistics and English Teaching at University College, London. Formerly headmaster of a primary school in London.

MARCKWARDT, ALBERT H. Professor of English and Linguistics, Princeton University, is president of NCTE and former president of the Linguistic Society of America and the American Dialect Society. Coauthor of *Facts About Current English Usage* and *A Common Language* and author of *Introduction to the English Language, American English,* and *Linguistics and the Teaching of English.* Director of the Dartmouth Seminar.

MILLER, JAMES E., JR. Professor of English, University of Chicago. Former editor of *College English* (1960–1966), and author of *Reader's Guide to Herman Melville, Walt Whitman,* and *Myth and Method: Theories of Modern Fiction.*

MOFFETT, JAMES P. Research Associate in English, Harvard Graduate School of Education (1966–1967). Former teacher of French and English at Phillips Exeter Academy. Coeditor of *Points of View: An Anthology of Short Stories.*

MUSCATINE, CHARLES. Professor of English, University of California, Berkeley. Specialist in medieval literature and culture and literary criticism. Publications include *The Book of Geoffrey Chaucer* and *The Borzoi College Reader.* Editor of *Education at Berkeley: Report of the Select Committee on Education.*

OLSON, PAUL A. Professor of English, University of Nebraska; Director of the Nebraska Curriculum Study Center in English. Has written on such varied topics as Gothic architecture, medieval exegesis, transformational grammar, and Ezra Pound. Author of *The Arts of Language* and *A Curriculum for English.*

O'NEIL, WAYNE A. Associate Professor of Education and Linguistics, Harvard University. Former Associate Director of the Oregon Curriculum Study Center. Author of *Kernels and Transformations.*

ROBSON, WALLACE. Fellow of Lincoln College, University of Oxford. Author of the recently published volume of literary criticism, *Critical Essays.*

ROSEN, CONNIE. Lecturer in Education at Goldsmiths College, University of London. Formerly headmistress of a primary school in London.

ROSEN, HAROLD. Lecturer in Education at the University of London Institute of Education. Has taught in grammar schools, comprehensive schools, and a college of education.

SINCLAIR, JOHN. Professor of Modern English Language, University of Birmingham. Has taught linguistics in the University of Edinburgh.

SQUIRE, JAMES R. Executive Secretary, NCTE, and Professor of English, University of Illinois. Coauthor of *The Teaching of Language and Literature* and other books, he has taught English in all secondary grades and is the Director of the National Study of High School English Programs and the Study of High School English Programs in Great Britain.

STRANG, BARBARA. Professor of English Language and General Linguistics, University of Newcastle upon Tyne. Author of *Modern English Structure.*

SUMMERFIELD, GEOFFREY. Lecturer in Education and English at the University of York. Formerly head of the English Department at Churchfields Comprehensive School near Birmingham. Author of *Topics in English.*

THOMPSON, DENYS. Editor of *The Use of English* since its foundation in 1948. Formerly headmaster of the grammar school at Yeovil and one of the editors of *Scrutiny.* Author of *Reading and Discrimination, The Voice of Civilization,* and *Between the Lines.* Vice-chairman of NATE 1965–1966.

WHITEHEAD, FRANK. Senior Lecturer in English and Education at the University of Sheffield Institute of Education. Former grammar school teacher; author of *The Disappearing Dais.* Chairman of NATE 1965–1967.

WHITTEMORE, REED. Poet and staff member of the National Institute of Public Affairs. Formerly Consultant in Poetry to the Library of Congress and Professor of English, Carleton College. Collected work in *The Self Made Man, The Boy from Iowa,* and *The Fascination of the Abomination.*

WILT, MIRIAM E. Professor of Early Childhood and Elementary Education, Temple University. Author of *Creativity in the Elementary School* and "Using the Implications of Linguistics to Improve the Teaching of English Language Arts in the Elementary School."

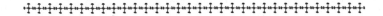

CONSULTANTS AT
THE DARTMOUTH SEMINAR

BALFOUR, DOROTHY K. Elementary School Teacher, McKee Elementary School, Edmonton, Alberta.

BERNSTEIN, BASIL BERNARD. Reader in the Sociology of Education, University of London Institute of Education.

CAWS, PETER J. Chairman, Department of Philosophy, Hunter College of the City University of New York, and Consultant, Carnegie Corporation of New York.

CORBIN, RICHARD. Chairman, English Department, Hunter College High School, and President of NCTE, 1965.

CROSBY, MURIEL. Assistant Superintendent for Educational Programs, Wilmington, Delaware, and President of NCTE, 1966.

EVERTTS, ELDONNA L. Assistant Executive Secretary, NCTE, and Associate Professor of Education, University of Illinois.

FISHMAN, JOSHUA A. University Research Professor of Social Sciences, Yeshiva University.

HARRIS, ROBIN S. Principal, Innis College, and Professor of Higher Education, University of Toronto.

HAZARD, PATRICK D. Chairman, English Department, Beaver College.

HOGAN, ROBERT F. Associate Executive Secretary, NCTE.

MCTEAGUE, FRANK. Head of English Department, Mimico High School, Toronto, Ontario.

MARCATANTE, JOHN J. Chairman, English Department, Astonia Junior High School, Toronto, Ontario.

MARKLE, SUSAN MEYER. Professor of Psychology, Bureau of Instructional Resources, University of Illinois, Chicago Circle.

MARSHALL, SYBIL. Lecturer in Primary Education, Institute of Education, University of Sheffield.

MINER, WALTER H. Teacher of English, East High School, Cheyenne, Wyoming.

ONG, WALTER J., S.J. Professor of English, Saint Louis University.

PARKER, HARLEY W. Head of Design, Royal Ontario Museum, University of Toronto.

PIPER, HENRY DAN. Dean, College of Liberal Arts and Sciences, Southern Illinois University.

PURVES, ALAN C. Associate Examiner in the Humanities, Educational Testing Service.

SAUNDERS, DOROTHY O. Elementary School Teacher, Brookmont Elementary School, Bethesda, Maryland.

SHUGRUE, MICHAEL F. Assistant Secretary for English, MLA.

WORK, WILLIAM. Executive Secretary, Speech Association of America.